HOME SKILLS

Ceramic Tile

HOW TO INSTALL CERAMIC TILE FOR YOUR FLOORS, WALLS, BACKSPLASHES & COUNTERTOPS

COOL
SPRINGS
PRESS
Home and Garden Experts™

MINNEAPOLIS, MINNESOTA

CONTENTS

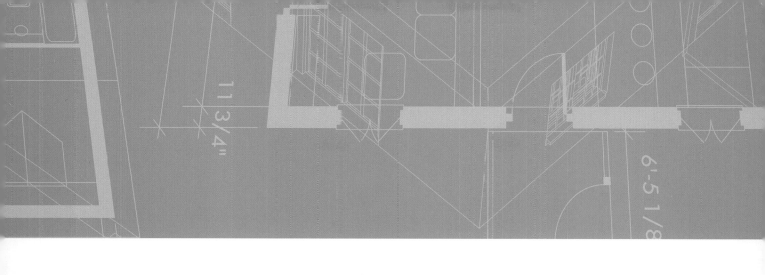

Tiling Floors

Tiling Walls

Tiling Countertops & Backsplashes

Tiling Outdoors

Resources

Introduction

TILES ARE AN ANCIENT building material with incredible durability. Mosaics from thousands of years ago still tell their stories beautifully. In many ways the tiles of today are very similar to tiles of the past hundred years. The techniques, however, have changed, and it is very possible to learn to set tile. Wouldn't it be wonderful to have such a long lasting surface in your own home?

But choosing and buying tile and tiling materials can be a daunting task. *HomeSkills: Ceramic Tile* has sections on the qualities and types of tile available for walls and floors that answer questions about durability, application, and appropriateness for various surfaces. Also covered is how to estimate the amounts of materials needed.

Though tile might be durable, it must be installed properly to take advantage of its strength. *HomeSkills: Ceramic Tile* provides all the information you need to evaluate and remove old surfaces, prepare substrates, and cut, set, and grout tile. By following step-by-step directions with clear photographs, you will learn all the skills necessary to complete the floor, wall, kitchen, and outdoor projects in this book. With the skills you develop, you can easily set off on your own creative tiling venture.

It can be nerve wracking to approach a large project like tiling a floor or tub surround. There are many steps to follow and care must be taken along the way. But tiling really is a skill within reach of any moderately handy person. Can you measure accurately and color within the lines? If yes, you can install tile successfully. Because of the nature of the material and the installation process, tiling can be done at your own pace. If you make an error, it is not difficult to back up and re-do the work.

Also included in *HomeSkills: Ceramic Tile* are Skillbuilder exercises. These are suggested practice activities you can do before undertaking a large project. By practicing on small, inconsequential projects, you gain an idea of your strengths and weaknesses. Don't be afraid to play around and experience failure with these little Skillbuilders. The more you learn from the Skillbuilders, the better your big, serious projects will turn out.

TILE BASICS

AT ITS MOST BASIC LEVEL, tile is any one of a number of materials designed to be cemented to a substrate and surrounded by grout. Tile may be porcelain, fired clay, cut stone, metal, glass, or cement. Tiles are available in sizes ranging from ¼-inch square mosaic tiles to 24- or 36-inch floor tiles. Some tiles are suitable for hard use in floors, while others are strictly for decorative purposes.

Knowing the difference is important and will improve your odds of creating a successful tile installation.

This chapter covers the types and styles of tile available today, and all the materials and tools you will need for a variety of tile projects. How to properly use the tools and materials is also included. You will learn the various ways to cut tile, from scoring and snapping to cutting with a wet saw.

BUY TILE & MATERIALS

Before you can select or purchase materials, you'll need to figure out exactly what you need and how much. Start by drawing a room layout, a reference for you and for anyone advising you about the project.

To estimate the amount of tile you need for a floor project, calculate the square footage of the room and add five percent for waste. For example, in a 10-foot × 12-foot room, the total area is 120 square feet. Add five percent, six square feet, for breakage and other waste. You'll need to purchase enough tile to cover 126 square feet

Tile cartons generally indicate the number of square feet one carton will cover. Divide the square footage to be covered by the square footage contained in a carton in order to determine the number of cartons required for your floor project. For example, if a carton holds 10 square feet, you will need 13 cartons to cover the 10 × 12 floor in our example.

Estimating tile for a wall project is slightly more complex. Start by deciding how much of each wall will be tiled. In a shower, plan to tile to at least six inches above the showerhead. It's common for tile to extend four feet up the remaining bathroom walls, although it's possible and sometimes very attractive for full walls to be tiled.

To calculate the amount of field tile required, measure each wall and multiply the width times the height of the area to be covered. Subtract the square footage of doors and windows. Do this for each wall, then add all the figures together to calculate the total square footage. Add five percent for waste. Calculate the number of cartons necessary (square footage of the project divided by the square footage contained in a carton).

Trim for floors and walls is sold by the lineal foot. Measure the lineal footage and calculate based on that. Plan carefully—the cost of trim tile adds up

quickly. See page 13 for further information on trim types and styles.

Before buying the tiles, ask about your dealer's return policy. Most dealers allow you to return unused tiles for a refund. In any case, think of it this way: buying a few too many tiles is a small problem. Running out of tiles before the job's done could turn into disaster if you can no longer get the tile or the colors don't match.

Example of Estimating Tile Needs

Wall 1: 8 × 8 ft. = 64.00 sq. ft. – (door 2.5 × 6.5 ft. = 16.25 sq. ft.) = 47.75 sq. ft.
+ Wall 2: 8 × 10 ft. = 80.00 sq. ft.
+ Wall 3: 8 × 8 ft. = 64.00 sq. ft. – (window 2 × 4 ft. = 8.00 sq. ft.) = 56.00 sq. ft.
+ Wall 4: 4 × 10 ft. = 40.00 sq. ft.

Total wall coverage =	223.75 sq. ft.
+ 5% waste	11.18 sq. ft.
New total tile needs	235.00 sq. ft.
÷ Amount of tile per carton (carton sizes vary)	10 sq. ft.
= Number of cartons needed	24 cartons

Mix tile from carton to carton. Slight variations in color won't be as noticeable mixed throughout the project as they would be if the color shifts from one area to another.

FLOOR TILE

Floor tile needs to be more than just attractive—it needs to be strong and durable as well. After all, floors bear the weight of furniture, foot traffic, and the sudden impact of every one and every thing that falls on them. Floor tile is engineered to tolerate these stresses. Most floor tile is also suitable for countertops. And although it's generally thicker and heavier than wall tile, many styles of floor tile can be used on walls. The trim pieces necessary for counters and walls aren't always available, though, which may limit your options.

When shopping for tile, look for ratings by the American National Standards Institute or the Porcelain Enamel Institute (see below). If ratings aren't available, check with your dealer to make sure the tile you're considering is suitable for your project.

Before you start shopping, consider where the tile will be used and what you want it to accomplish. Will it be exposed to moisture? Should it be a focal point or a subtle background? Do you want the floor to establish the room's color scheme or blend into it? The range of options is truly mind-boggling, so establish some guidelines before you go shopping to simplify the selection process.

Floor Tile Ratings

Floor tile often comes labeled with water absorption and Porcelain Enamel Institute (PEI) ratings. Ratings indicate how a tile can be used and whether or not it needs to be sealed against moisture. Absorption is a concern because tile that soaks up water is susceptible to mildew and mold and can be difficult to clean. Tile is rated non-vitreous, semi-vitreous, vitreous, or impervious, in increasing order of water resistance. Non-vitreous tile is quite porous; semi-vitreous is used in dry-to-occasionally-wet locations; vitreous tile can be used without regard to its exposure to moisture. Impervious tile is generally reserved for restaurants, hospitals, and commercial applications where sanitation is a special concern.

The PEI number is a wear rating that indicates how the tile should be used. Ratings of 1 and 2 indicate tile is suitable for walls only; tile rated 3

and 4 is suitable for all residential applications—walls, counters, and floors. Most tile carries absorption and PEI ratings, but some, especially imported and art tiles, may not. Ask the retailer if you're not sure.

Depending on the retailer, tile may also have other ratings. Some tile is graded 1 to 3 for the quality of manufacturing. Grade 1 indicates standard grade; 2 indicates minor glaze and size flaws; 3 indicates major flaws; use for decoration only. Tile suitable for outdoor use is sometimes rated with regard to its resistance to frost. Finally, coefficient of friction numbers may be included with some tile. The higher the coefficient, the more slip resistant the tile. A dry coefficient of .6 is the minimum standard established by the Americans with Disabilities Act.

Floor tiles are thicker and almost always larger than wall tiles. Ceramic floor tiles are usually between ¼ and ½" thick.

WALL TILE

Wall tile, unlike floor tile, doesn't have the burden of bearing weight or withstanding heavy traffic, so it can be thinner, have finer finishes, and, in some cases, be less expensive. Wall tile layouts tend to have more exposed edges, so manufacturers often offer matching trim and border pieces with finished edges. Wall tile is generally self spacing—individual tiles have small flanges on each edge to help keep the spacing even. You can use floor tile on walls, but since it is heavier, it tends to slide down during installation. Using battens while installing can help solve this problem. Fewer styles of matching trim tile are available for floor tile, which may make it difficult to conceal unfinished edges.

Wall tile should not be used on floors or countertops, however, because it will not stand up to much weight or sudden impacts. If you have concerns about a tile's suitability for your application, ask your retailer or look for ratings by the American National Standards Institute or the Porcelain Enamel Institute. Wall tile can be a fairly inconspicuous wall covering or, if used in an elaborate design, can become the focal point of a room. As with floor tiles, there are styles for every effect from subtle to bold, so envision the effect you want before you head to the tile store or home improvement center.

Wall Tile Ratings

Most tile intended for walls comes labeled with a water absorption rating. As with floor tile, absorbent wall tile will be susceptible to mildew and mold and be difficult to clean. Tiles are rated non-vitreous, semi-vitreous, vitreous, and impervious, in increasing order of water resistance. Practically speaking, these ratings tell you whether your tile may require sealant or if it can be left as is. Non-vitreous and semi-vitreous do absorb noticeable amounts of water and may need to be sealed in damp rooms like bathrooms. Sealant can alter a tile's appearance, so test before you buy.

There are a few other ratings to consider when purchasing wall tile. Depending on where you buy tile, it may be graded from 1 to 3 for the quality of manufacturing. Grade 1 indicates standard grade, suitable for all installations. Grade 2 indicates minor glaze and size flaws, but the tile is structurally standard. Grade 3 tiles may be slightly irregular in shape and are decorative, suitable only for walls. Tiles with manufacturing irregularities may be more difficult to lay out and install precisely. If you live in a freeze zone and are looking for tile for outdoor walls, you'll also want tile rated resistant to frost. If the frost-resistance rating is not on the package, the retailer should be able to tell you. Some colored tile may come with a graphic to indicate the degree of color variation from tile to tile—in most cases it will vary somewhat.

Wall tiles are usually less than ¼" thick and no larger than 6 × 6", with 4 × 4" tiles the most common. Lightweight tiles are less likely to sag during installation.

TYPES OF TILE

Porcelain tile (right) is produced by pressing refined clay into shape and then firing it in a kiln at very high temperatures. The resulting tile is extremely hard, absorbs very little or no water, and doesn't stain or mildew. Porcelain tile is manufactured in all shapes and sizes, and, because its white base color accepts dye beautifully, a virtually unlimited range of colors and finishes are available. Tile makers can also imprint textures when the tile is pressed to create a slip-resistant surface well suited for floors in wet locations. Porcelain tile is colored by mixing dye into the clay rather than applying it in a glaze, which means the color extends through the full thickness of the tile. Because of this process, tile makers can press finer, more intricate textures and patterns into the tile. Porcelain tile can even be pressed so that it's nearly indistinguishable from cut stone, which tends to be more expensive but less durable. For ease of care, porcelain is hard to beat. Its smooth finish and imperviousness to moisture keep soil and stains from setting in, making it easy to maintain. Note: grout can stain porous material, so take great care in grouting and be sure to follow manufacturer instructions.

Glazed ceramic tile (left) is made from clay pressed into a shape by a machine, glazed, and then fired in a kiln. The glaze, made up of a number of glass and metal elements, provides color and creates a hard, shiny surface. To make floor tile slip-resistant, the surface can be textured, given a slightly raised design, or the glaze itself may include materials added to create a non-skid surface. Glazed tile generally absorbs very little or no water, making it both easy to maintain and mildew resistant. If the glaze is hard and scratch-resistant and the tile is properly installed and maintained, glazed ceramic tile can last for decades.

Metal tiles are quite expensive per square foot, but adding just a few to an installation of glazed or porcelain tiles can have a big impact. Metal tiles are installed just like standard tiles, and they are available in shapes and thicknesses to work in most layouts. They are available with smooth finishes, polished or unpolished, and with embossed designs. Some metals may weather and discolor with time and exposure to moisture.

Glass tile is an especially interesting option for walls, although in some applications it can be used on floors as well. It is available in a variety of colors, degrees of translucency, shapes, and sizes. Because most glass tile is translucent to some degree, it's important to use a white tile adhesive that won't affect the appearance of the tiles once they are installed. Glass is impervious to moisture, but can be scratched and cracked, so it shouldn't be installed where it will get hit by swinging doors or scratched by general traffic.

Natural stone tile is marble, granite, slate, and other more exotic stones cut very precisely into tiles of various sizes that can be installed just like manufactured tile. Because stone is a natural material, variations in color, texture, and markings must be expected. Manufacturers do offer stone tiles with some added finish. In addition to polished tile, suppliers offer a variety of distressed and textured finishes that can be very attractive as well as slip-resistant. With the exception of granite, natural stone tends to be quite porous and requires periodic sealing to prevent staining. Also, not all types are uniformly abrasion-resistant, so check before making a purchase. Some stone is so soft that it can be very easily scratched by normal use.

Terra-cotta tile evokes images of rustic patios in Mexico or perhaps sunny piazzas on the Mediterranean. These images are quite appropriate because terra-cotta tile originated in these regions. The tile is traditionally made by pressing unrefined clay into molds of various shapes and firing it (terra-cotta literally means "baked earth"). The color of the tile, from brown to red to yellow, is largely a result of the minerals unique to the local soil. Machine-made terra-cotta tile is regular in shape and can be laid like standard tile, but traditional terra-cotta, especially handmade Mexican saltillo tile, has irregularities and uneven shapes and thus requires more care during installation. The variability and rustic character of the tile make up much of its appeal—and terra-cotta can be quite slip-resistant. Unglazed terra-cotta, which is porous and absorbent, should be treated with sealant before being used in wet locations.

Mosaic tiles are ceramic, porcelain, terra-cotta, stone, or other tile cut into small pieces. Individual small tiles are often mounted on a mesh backing so that large squares of many tiles can be installed at once. These squares may be a solid color or contain a pattern or image. Individual mosaic tiles are also available for making custom accents and mosaics. Mosaic tile can be very low maintenance or it can require periodic application of sealant, depending on the material. Mosaic tile is generally quite slip-resistant because of the large number of grout lines in an installation.

Cement body tiles are actually shaped pieces of concrete. They can be made in nearly endless colors and textures because cement can be dyed, coated, and molded quite easily. It can even be finished to take on the appearance of marble or other stone. Cement tile can also be pressed with pronounced raised or relief designs. Cement tile is an economical choice both for its low cost and great durability, but there are several factors to keep in mind. Unfinished cement tile is highly porous and stains very easily. Some cement tile is unsuitable for outdoor installations, as it may crack if it freezes. Cement tile should be treated periodically with a sealant to preserve its appearance and prevent mildew.

Trim tiles are designed to conceal exposed edges of field tile, especially on wall and counter installations. Bullnose tile is used to finish the edges of partial walls; cove and corner tile shields curves and corners; chair rail tile accents a wall of field tile or functions as an accent around edges. When planning a wall project, investigate available trim as part of the planning process.

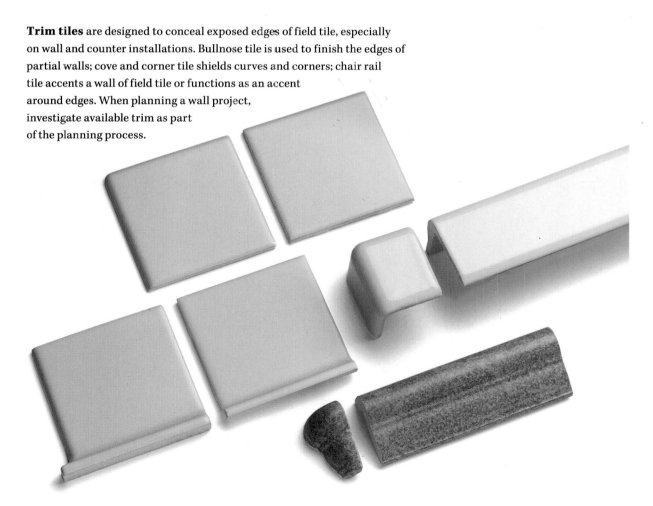

MATERIALS: LEVELERS & RESURFACERS

Self-leveling underlayment, otherwise referred to as self-leveling cement, is applied over uneven surfaces, such as cementitious backers and concrete slabs, to make them level prior to tile application. A similar product called concrete resurfacer accomplishes essentially the same thing. Levelers and resurfacers have fairly liquid viscosities. They are poured onto uneven surfaces, where gravity directs them to fill in the low areas of a subfloor. One 50-pound bag of floor leveler will typically cover a surface area of approximately 50 square feet, at ⅛-inch thick. Leveler can be applied in layers as thin as a feather edge and as thick as one inch, depending on the specific product you buy. Self-leveling underlayment cures very quickly,

usually within a few hours of application. In some cases, multiple applications are required to build up to the desired thickness.

A coat of paint-like primer should be applied prior to the leveler in almost all cases. This is usually rolled onto the substrate using a short-nap roller. The primer seals the substrate, which helps keep it from absorbing the moisture in the cement mixture too rapidly. It also improves the adhesive bond between the self-leveling cement and the surface it is applied to.

The leveler compound is best mixed using a ½-inch corded drill fitted with a mixing paddle. A garden rake and a trowel will also be necessary to spread the batch over the area in need of repair.

Cement-based tile products such as this floor leveler must be mixed well with water. A ½" power drill with a mixing paddle attachment is a great help in this regard.

Floor levelers and resurfacers are applied prior to installing tile backer to address dips, valleys, and other uneven areas in a concrete floor. An acrylic or latex fortifier helps the product flow more smoothly and gives it some extra flex, without sacrificing hardness.

1. Patch any major cracks or large popouts with concrete patching compound before you apply the leveler. Once the patch dries, wash and rinse the floor according to the instructions on the leveler package. This may include the use of grease cutters and pressure washers.

2. Apply an even layer of concrete primer to the entire surface using a long-nap paint roller. Let the primer dry completely.

3. Following the manufacturer's instructions, mix the floor leveler with water. The batch should be large enough to cover the entire floor area to the desired thickness (up to 1"). Pour the leveler over the floor.

4. Distribute the leveler evenly, using a rake or spreader. Work quickly: the leveler begins to harden in 15 min. Use a trowel to feather the edges and create a smooth transition with an uncovered area. Let the leveler dry for 24 hrs.

MATERIALS: TILE BACKER

Tile backer is any approved sheet panel that is installed on subfloor, countertop, or wall surface to serve as underlayment for the installation of tiles. Most commonly today, that means cementboard. Cementboard was invented in the early 1960s by Paul Dinkel, a tile contractor determined to develop a tile substrate to replace drywall, which is prone to deterioration in wet areas. His solution was a thin, precast, strong concrete-base panel that has come to be known as cementboard.

The projects in this book employ cement and fiber/cement backer boards. They are commonly sold in three-by-five-foot panels in thickness of ½-inch or ¼-inch. For walls, ½-inch-thick backer board is installed over wall studs spaced 16 inches on center. For horizontal applications (floors, countertops, and tub decks), either ¼- or ½-inch-thick cementboard may be used. For floors, the joists should be spaced 16 inches on center and there should be a subbase of ¾-inch thick sheathing. Unless otherwise allowed by the manufacturer, use ½-inch-thick cementboard for all other applications.

On horizontal surfaces, the backer board panel may be laminated to the subbase using a dry-set or modified thinset mortar bed and then fastened with screws or nails. This setting bed is required by some local codes, but may not be required in your area. It is a good idea regardless, as it eliminates voids under the panels and provides a dimensionally stable surface for the application of tile. This greatly reduces tile cracking.

Proper fastener selection is critical for the long-term success of any backer board installation. Use 1¼-inch, corrosion-resistant backer board screws with a minimum of a ⅜-inch diameter head. A full-sized backer board panel installed over a floor or countertop will require up to 60 screws. Wall applications will require up to 30 screws per panel, and ceiling applications will require up to 42 screws per panel.

Alkaline resistant, two-inch-wide fiberglass mesh tape is used in conjunction with a modified thinset mortar to reinforce the adjoining edges between backer board panels. Fiberglass tapes that are not alkaline resistant will degrade over time, become brittle, and lose their reinforcing strength.

Tile backer board is designed to retain its rigidity when damp—whether the dampness is from the thinset mortar during the application or the conditions of the room. Cement or fiber/cement base backer (cementboard) is made in ¼ and ½" thicknesses. Other fiberglass-base tile backers are lighter than cementboard and some installers find them easier to work with.

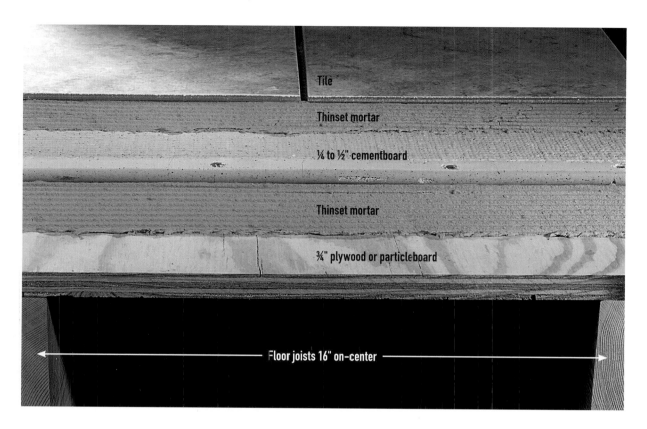

Tile

Thinset mortar

¼ to ½" cementboard

Thinset mortar

¾" plywood or particleboard

Floor joists 16" on-center

A typical tile floor has floor joists spaced 16" on center, topped with a subbase of ¾" plywood or particleboard sheathing. A layer of cementboard (you may use ¼ or ½") is set into a bed of thinset mortar (in most cases) and fastened down with cementboard screws. The tile flooring is laid into another bed of thinset on top of the cementboard.

Cementboard screws are specially designed to penetrate the cementitious material without cracking it.

Cementboard mesh tape is used to cover and reinforce the seams between cementboard panels. Don't use regular mesh tapes for this job: they are not alkali-resistant and will degrade.

MATERIALS: TILE MEMBRANES

Tile membranes are thin, flexible tile underlayment materials designed to isolate tile installations from problematic substrates, provide for sound abatement, or waterproof and vapor-proof tile installations in wet areas and steam rooms. There are dozens of different types of tile membranes on the market. Please refer to the manufacturer for specific information pertaining to the limitations, benefits, and installation of the membrane selected.

Waterproofing membranes are installed in wet areas and are designed to prevent the migration of water beyond the membrane. They often provide additional benefits, including crack suppression. Tile installed in steam rooms, wet saunas, and steam showers requires the installation of a membrane that is both vapor-proof and waterproof.

Sound isolation membranes are designed to reduce the transmission of impact sounds from hard surface flooring to lower level living spaces. This type of membrane is usually installed in apartment dwellings and condominiums (and behind drywall in home theaters).

Crack isolation and anti-fracture membranes, also called crack suppression membranes, isolate tile installations from tile substrates that are susceptible to stresses that produce horizontal movement. They can absorb movement of as much as ⅛-inch to ⅜-inch. Some membranes are liquid applied to the substrate with a trowel or roller, others are sheet applied. There are even anti-fracture thinset mortars, eliminating the need in some cases, for a separate sheet or liquid applied membrane.

Uncoupling membranes isolate the finished tile installation from the substrate while allowing both to move independently. This type of membrane is typically installed over problematic sub-floors and newly installed or problematic concrete slabs.

Crack suppression and uncoupling membranes are not intended to be a substitution for sound building practices. Tile installations that exceed structural recommendations may see little benefit with the installation of these types of products. Likewise, marginal installations will benefit more from structural reinforcement or repairs. Whenever possible, reinforce weak wall framing and floor joists with wood blocking and install an additional layer of plywood over wood sub-floors if needed.

Membranes used for laying tile include: Roll-on waterproofing and crack prevention membrane (A); crack prevention mat (B); multi-purpose membrane for uncoupling, waterproofing and vapor management (C); 40-mil thick (1/16") self-bonding membrane designed for use under floor tile requiring protection from structural movement (D); 40-mil thick PVC shower pan liner (E).

MATERIALS: TILE TRANSITION STRIPS

Available in numerous materials and profiles, transition strips are installed to create a smooth bridge from one floor covering to another. They are typically installed in doorways or in any open area where a newly installed tile floor will abut another floor covering. The type of profile required will depend largely on the floor surfaces being transitioned. Height reducing thresholds, or reducer strips, have a profile with a beveled edge and are used to transition between two floors of differing height. Gradual transition strips have a sloped profile, making them wheelchair friendly. T-molding is used to transition between two floors of even height. Transition strips can often be omitted on transitions between carpet and tile.

Usually found in doorways, transition strips are installed after the tile layout is completed to create a bridge between floor coverings. Individual strips are engineered for specific transitions: for example, ceramic tile to hardwood or tile to carpeting.

Carpet is usually tucked right up to the edge of a tile installation.

Carpet can also be tucked into a threshold, as shown here.

T-molding is used to transition between two floors of even height.

Transition strips with an edge profile do not have a height adjusting profile. They are used to protect the edges of exposed tile.

Height reducing thresholds are used to transition between two floors of differing heights.

To make a room accessible to wheelchair users, use a gradual transition strip with a sloped profile.

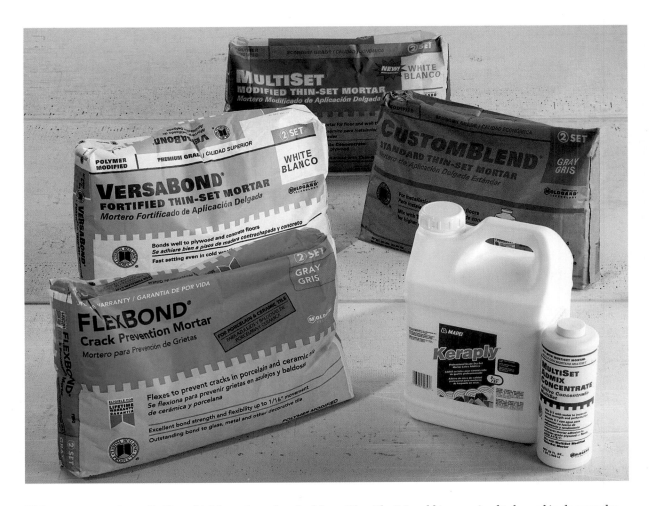

Thinset mortar is applied in a thick layer to make a bed for setting tile. It is sold in premixed tubs and in dry powder forms—most professionals prefer to mix their own. If the product you buy has not been modified with polymer additive, you can mix in latex additive yourself. Different thinset mortars have different ratios of additives and fortifiers for specific purposes. You will also find some color variation. Most is cement gray, but white thinset intended for use with glass tile is also available. You can also use white thinset to reduce the chance of color bleedthrough if you are applying a light-colored grout.

Polymer-modified thinset mortar contains dry-polymer additives. It also should be mixed with potable water. Latex-modified thinset is prepared by mixing dry-set thinset mortar with a liquid latex additive. Although more costly and difficult to work with than conventional modified blends, liquid latex modified mortars usually offer higher bond strengths, higher flexural values, and increased water and chemical resistance.

Small quantities of mortar can be mixed by hand to a smooth and creamy consistency using a margin trowel. Larger batches of mortar can be mixed at speeds of less than 300 rpm, using a ½-inch drill fitted with a mixing paddle.

Cementboard setting beds are applied using a ¼-inch square notch trowel. Use a ¼-inch V-notch trowel to install mosaic tiles two inches square or less. Most varieties of larger tile can be installed using a ¼-inch or ⅜-inch square or U-notch trowel. Very large tiles and certain types of stone may require larger trowel sizes.

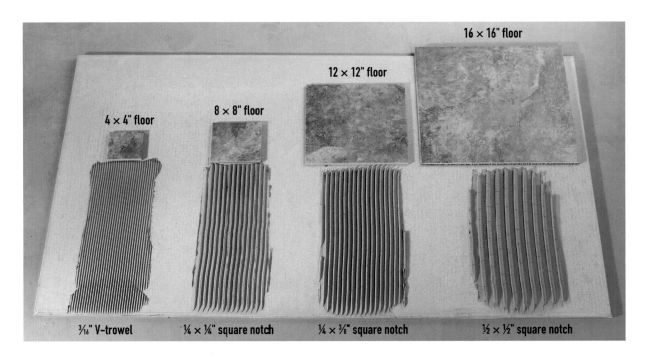

16 × 16" floor

12 × 12" floor

8 × 8" floor

4 × 4" floor

³⁄₁₆" V-trowel   ¼ × ¼" square notch   ¼ × ⅜" square notch   ½ × ½" square notch

The type of trowel used to apply thinset is dictated mostly by the size of the tile being installed.

Introduced in the early 1950s, thinset is an adhesive mortar consisting of Portland cement, a water retentive agent, sand or aggregate (optional), and other additives. Prior to thinset, tiles were installed with a thick paste consisting of Portland cement and water. Unless they were soaked in water prior to installation, absorbent tiles would quickly soak up the moisture in the paste and fail to bond to the substrate. Thinset mortar made it possible for installers to install tile over a variety of cementitious substrates without needing to soak the tile beforehand.

Thinset mortars have improved substantially in quality and ease of use over the years. Because no two products are exactly alike, you should always read the package label carefully to make sure the product you select is an appropriate adhesive for the tile and the substrate to which it will be applied.

The adhesive mortars used for the projects in this book include dry-set thinset mortar, polymer-modified thinset mortar, and latex-modified thinset mortar. Modified thinset, the most common adhesive used, is widely employed to adhere a variety of different types of tile to cementboard and concrete substrates. Use gray thinset for darker grout selections and white thinset for lighter grout selections.

Dry-set mortars are mixed with potable water and used as a setting bed to seat backer board panels. In special circumstances, it can also be used as an adhesive to set tile.

If you are only tiling a small area, consider buying tubs of premixed thinset mortar. It is more expensive than the dry mix, but it is convenient. Not only that, you are assured that the material contains an adequate ratio of latex additive and is blended to the proper consistency.

MATERIALS: GROUT

Grout (or "grout mortar") is available in dozens of stock colors and can be tinted to an unlimited variety of tones. Beyond color, grout has several other features that differ, making some types more appropriate for various applications than others.

The projects in this book use polymer-modified grout or dry-set grout mixed with a liquid latex additive. Polymer-modified grout contains an additive in dry form that is activated when mixed with water. Latex-modified grout is prepared by mixing a dry-set grout with a liquid latex additive. These additives aid in increasing the water and chemical resistance, bonding, and compressive strength of the grout.

To apply grout to floor or wall tile installations, a rubber grout float is needed, along with a minimum of one or two large grout sponges for every 150 square feet of tile installed. A margin trowel is also useful for spreading grout under kitchen or bathroom cabinet toe kicks and other hard-to-reach areas.

A few days after installation, a water-based silicone grout sealer may be applied to finished grout joints. Keep in mind, these types of sealers will not waterproof the grout. They are designed to be vapor transmissive and allow moisture to evaporate from the surface of the grout joint. Grout sealers do help to prevent some mild blemishing and, at the very least, they allow for a little leeway for cleaning up spills before they have time to permanently stain the grout.

Tip

The spacing of the tiles will determine the type of grout to be applied. Unsanded grout is used with grout joints ⅛" wide or narrower. Sanded grout is used for grout joints that will be wider than ⅛".

Remember to treat any gaps between the tile and walls, tubs, cabinets, and other hard surfaces as expansion joints. Do not apply grout in these areas. Instead, cover them with molding or fill them with a flexible, mildew-resistant silicone, urethane, or latex caulk.

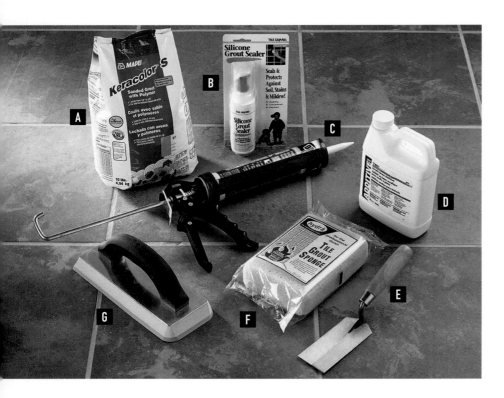

Materials and tools for grouting tile joints include: Dry mix, sanded grout (A); silicone grout sealer (B); tub-and-tile caulk (C); latex grout fortifier (D); margin trowel (E); grout sponge (F); grout float (G).

1   To make a small batch of mortar, add the proper ratio of water or liquid additive and dry powder to a container and stir by hand.

2   A heavy duty ½" drill fitted with a mixing paddle is useful for mixing large quantities of mortar at one time.

On the back of each bag of thinset mortar or grout you will find instructions detailing the amount of water or liquid additive required, slake time, mixing speeds, and other important guidelines. These recommendations should always be followed carefully. Any variation in the mixing guidelines can create problems, ranging from uneven or washed out grout colors, to weakened mortars that lack compressive strength or fail to adequately bond to tile and substrates.

To mix a full bag of mortar, add one half of the amount of potable water or liquid additive recommended by the manufacturer to a five gallon bucket. Slowly add a half bag of mortar while mixing the water and dry mix together with a ½-inch (chuck capacity) electric drill fitted with a mixing paddle.

Keep the paddle turning at a low rate. Repeat the process, mixing the entire batch thoroughly and uniformly for several minutes to a smooth, paste-like consistency.

If recommended by the manufacturer, allow the batch to slake. This is simply a waiting period that allows the dry mortar to more thoroughly absorb the liquid that was added to it. After the batch has slaked for the appropriate amount of time, mix the mortar once more and it will be ready for use.

Stiffened batches of thinset and grout mortars that have become too difficult to work with may be mixed again to loosen them up. However, this should be done without adding additional water or liquid additives.

TOOLS FOR REMOVING OLD SURFACES

Quality tools remove old surfaces faster and leave surfaces ready to accept new tile. Home centers and hardware stores carry a variety of products for surface removal. Look for tools with smooth, secure handles and correctly weighted heads for safety and comfort.

End-cutting nippers allow you to pull out staples remaining in the floor after carpeting is removed. This plier-like tool can also be used to break an edge on old tile so a chisel or pry bar can be inserted.

Heat guns are used to soften adhesives so vinyl base cove moldings and stubborn tiles can be pried away from the wall. They are also used to remove old paint, especially when it is heavily layered or badly chipped.

Hand mauls are often used in combination with pry bars and chisels to remove old flooring and prepare surfaces for tile. They are helpful for leveling high spots on concrete floors and separating underlayments and subfloors.

Flat pry bars are used to remove wood base moldings from walls and to separate underlayments and floor coverings from subfloors. This tool is also effective for removing tiles set in mortar.

Chisels come in a variety of sizes for specific jobs. Masonry chisels are used with hand mauls to remove high spots in concrete. Cold chisels are used with hand mauls or hammers to pry tiles from mortar.

Floor scrapers are used to scrape and smooth patched areas on concrete floors, and to pry up flooring, and scrape adhesives and backings from underlayments.

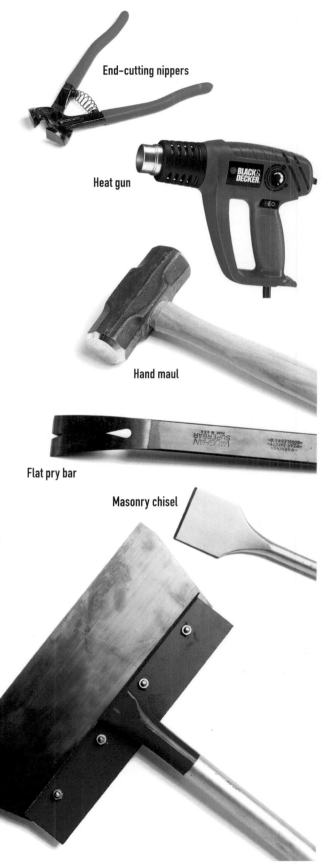

End-cutting nippers

Heat gun

Hand maul

Flat pry bar

Masonry chisel

Floor scraper

TOOLS FOR REPAIRING SUBSTRATES

Surfaces and substrates must be in good condition before new tile can be installed. Use the tools below to create stiff, flat surfaces that help prevent tiles from cracking and enhance the overall appearance of your finished project.

Straightedges are used to mark damaged areas of substrate for removal. They are also used to measure and mark replacement pieces for cutting.

Jigsaws are handy when cutting notches, holes, and irregular shapes in new or existing substrates. They are also used to fit new substrate pieces to existing doorways.

Portable drills secure substrates to subfloors with screws selected for the thickness and type of substrate used.

Circular saws are used to remove damaged sections of subfloor and cut replacement pieces to fit.

Straightedge

Portable drill

Jigsaw

Circular saw

TOOLS FOR INSTALLING SUBSTRATES

Depending upon your application, you may have to cut and install a substrate of cementboard, plywood, cork, backerboard, greenboard, or moisture membrane. Whichever your tiling project demands, the tools shown here will help you measure, score, cut, and install substrate material with precision.

Drywall squares are used to measure and mark substrates, such as cementboard, fiber-cementboard, and isolation membrane. They can also be used as straightedge guides for scoring and cutting substrates with a utility knife.

Utility knives are usually adequate for scoring straight lines in wallboard, cementboard, fiber-cementboard, and for cutting isolation membrane substrates. However, because cementboard and fiber-cementboard are thick, hard substrates, utility knife blades must be replaced often for best performance.

Cementboard knives are the best choice for scoring cementboard and fiber-cementboard. The blades on these knives are stronger and wear better than utility knife blades when cutting rough surfaces.

Trowels are useful for applying leveler on existing floors and for applying thinset mortar to substrates. Trowels can also be used to scrape away ridges and high spots after levelers or mortars dry.

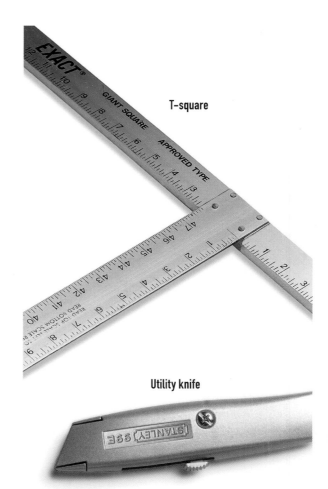

T-square

Utility knife

Cementboard knife

Notched trowel

TOOLS FOR LAYOUT

Laying tile requires careful planning. Since tile is installed following a grid-pattern layout, marking perpendicular reference lines is essential to proper placement. Use the tools shown here to measure and mark reference lines for any type of tiling project.

Straightedges are handy for marking reference lines on small areas. They can also be used to mark cutting lines for partial tiles.

Levels are used to check walls for plumb and horizontal surfaces for level before tile is laid. Levels are also used to mark layouts for wall tile installations.

Carpenter's squares are used to establish perpendicular lines for floor tile installations.

Chalk lines are snapped to mark the reference lines for layouts.

Tape measures are essential for measuring rooms and creating layouts. They're also used to make sure that reference lines are perpendicular by using the 3-4-5 triangle method.

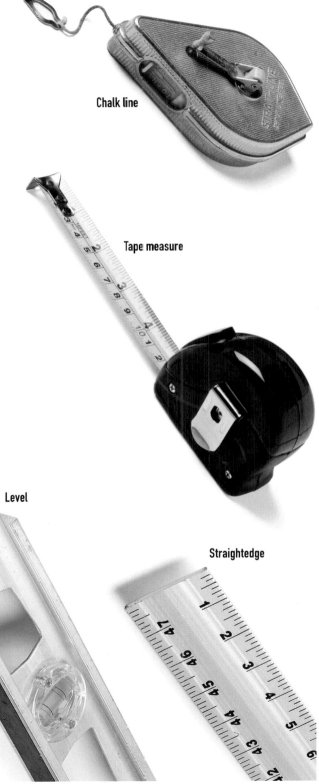

Chalk line

Tape measure

Carpenter's square

Level

Straightedge

TOOLS FOR CUTTING TILE

Even though tile is a rigid material, it can be cut to fit a variety of applications. With the proper tools, tile can be trimmed, notched, and drilled. If you're planning only one tile project, consider renting the more expensive pieces of equipment.

Coping saws with rod saw blades are usually adequate for cutting soft tile, such as wall tile.

Tile nippers are used to create curves and circles. Tile is first marked with the scoring wheel of a hand-held tile cutter or a wet saw blade to create a cutting guide.

Hand-held tile cutters are used to snap tiles one at a time. They are often used for cutting mosaic tiles after they have been scored.

Tile stones file away rough edges left by tile nippers and hand-held tile cutters. Stones can also be used to shave off small amounts of tile for fitting.

Wet saws, also called "tile saws," employ water to cool both the blade and the tile during cutting. This tool is used primarily for cutting floor tile—especially natural stone tile—but it is also useful for quickly cutting large quantities of tile or notches in hard tile.

Diamond blades are used on hand-held wet saws and grinders to cut through the hardest tile materials such as pavers, marble, granite, slate, and other natural stone.

Tile cutters are quick, efficient tools for scoring and cutting straight lines in most types of light- to medium-weight tile.

Grinders come in handy for cutting granite and marble when equipped with a diamond blade. Cuts made with this hand tool will be less accurate than with a wet saw, so it is best used to cut tile for areas that will be covered with molding or fixtures.

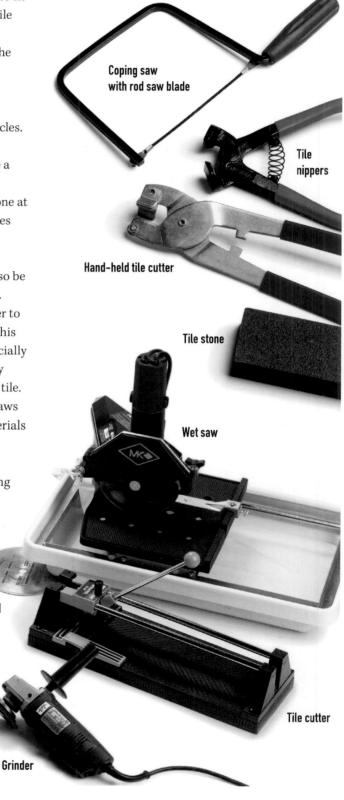

Coping saw with rod saw blade

Tile nippers

Hand-held tile cutter

Tile stone

Wet saw

Diamond blade

Tile cutter

Grinder

TOOLS FOR SETTING & GROUTING TILE

Laying tile requires quick, precise work, so it's wise to assemble the necessary supplies before you begin. You don't want to search for a tool with wet mortar already in place. Some of the tools required for setting and grouting tile are probably already in your tool box, so take an inventory before you head to the home center or hardware store.

Tile spacers are essential for achieving consistent spacing between tiles. They are set at corners of laid tile and are later removed so grout can be applied.

Grout sponges, buff rags, foam brushes, and grout sealer applicators are used after grout is applied. Grout sponges are used to wipe away grout residue, buff rags remove grout haze, and foam brushes and grout sealer applicators are for applying grout sealer.

Rubber mallets are used to gently tap tiles and set them evenly into mortar.

Needlenose pliers come in handy for removing spacers placed between tiles.

Caulk guns are used to fill expansion joints at the floor and base trim, at inside corners, and where tile meets surfaces made of other materials.

Grout floats are used to apply grout over tile and into joints. They are also used to remove excess grout from the surface of tiles after grout has been applied. For mosaic sheets, grout floats are handy for gently pressing tile into mortar.

Trowels are used to apply mortar to surfaces where tile will be laid and to apply mortar directly to the backs of cut tiles.

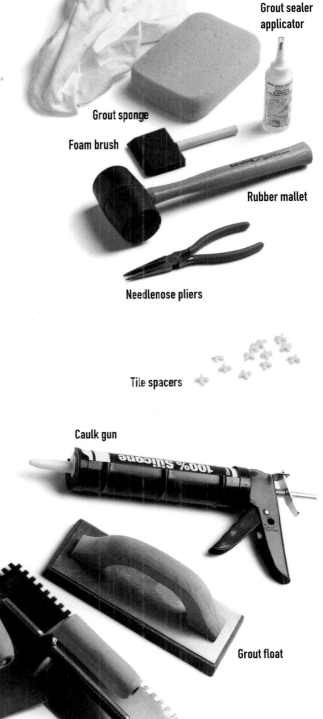

Buff rag

Grout sealer applicator

Grout sponge

Foam brush

Rubber mallet

Needlenose pliers

Tile spacers

Caulk gun

Trowel

Grout float

Notched trowel

CUTTING TILE

Careful planning will help you eliminate unnecessary cuts, but most tile jobs require cutting at least a few tiles and some jobs require cutting a large number of tiles, no matter how carefully you plan. For a few straight cuts on light- to medium-weight tile, use a snap cutter. If you're working with heavy tile or a large number of cuts on any kind of tile, a wet saw greatly simplifies the job. When using a wet saw, wear safety glasses and hearing protection. Make sure the blade is in good condition and the water container is full. Never use the saw without water, even for a few seconds.

Other cutting tools include nippers, hand-held tile cutters, and rod saws. Nippers can be used on most types of tile, but a rod saw is most effective with wall tile, which is generally fairly soft.

A note of caution: hand-held tile cutters and tile nippers can create razor-sharp edges. Handle freshly cut tile carefully, and immediately round over the edges with a tile stone.

Skillbuilder

Purchase some inexpensive floor and wall tiles. Practice making straight and curved cuts using the snap cutter, handheld tile cutters, and nippers. Rent a tile wet saw for an extra day before beginning your project and practice straight, notched, and round cuts. This may seem like an unnecessary extra expense, but time spent practicing before the project will save you energy and anxiety.

USING A SNAP CUTTER

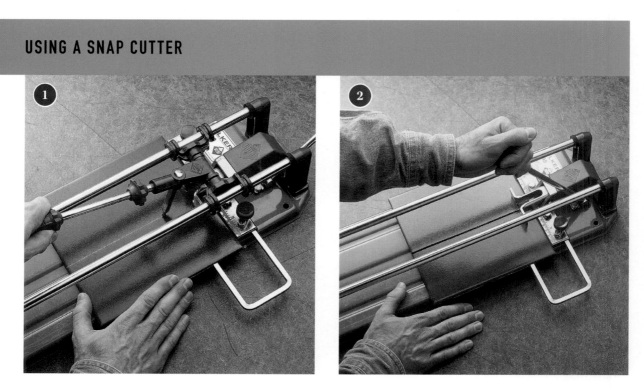

1   Mark a cutting line on the tile with a pencil, then place the tile in the cutter so the cutting wheel is directly over the line. While pressing down firmly on the wheel handle, run the wheel across the tile to score the surface. For a clean cut, score the tile only once.

2   Snap the tile along the scored line, as directed by the tool manufacturer. Usually, snapping the tile is accomplished by depressing a lever on the tile cutter.

USING A WET SAW

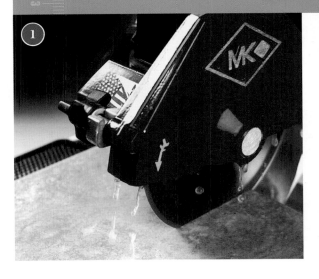

1 Individual saws vary, so read the manufacturer's directions for use and make sure you understand them. Refer any questions to the rental center. Wear safety glasses and hearing protection; make sure water is reaching the blade at all times.

2 Place the tile on the sliding table and lock the fence to hold the tile in place, then press down on the tile as you slide it past the blade.

MARKING SQUARE NOTCHES

1 Place the tile to be notched over the last full tile on one side of the corner. Set another full tile against the ½" spacer along the wall and trace along the opposite edge onto the second tile.

2 Move the top two tiles and spacer to the adjoining wall, making sure not to turn the tile that is being marked. Make a second mark on the tile as in step 1. Cut the tile and install.

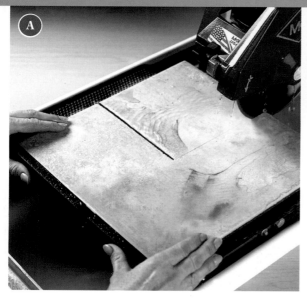

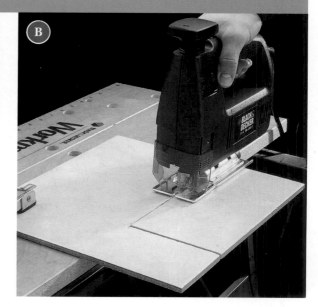

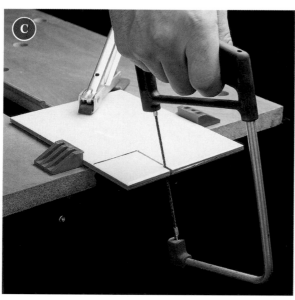

A   Cut along the marked line on one side of the notch. Turn the tile and cut along the other line to complete the notch. To keep the tile from breaking before you're through, slow down as you get close to the intersection with the first cut.

B   To cut square notches in a small number of wall tiles, clamp the tile down on a worktable, then use a jigsaw with a tungsten carbide blade to make the cuts. If you need to notch quite a few tiles, a wet saw is more efficient.

C   To make a small number of cuts in wall tile, you can use a rod saw. Fit a tungsten carbide rod saw into a hacksaw body. Firmly support the tile and use a sawing motion to cut the tile.

D   To make a very small notch, use tile nippers. Score the lines and then nibble up to the lines, biting very small pieces at a time.

MARKING & CUTTING IRREGULAR NOTCHES

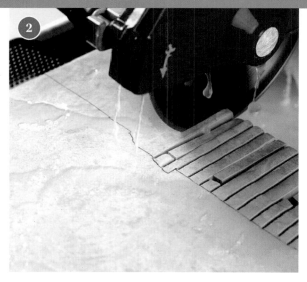

1   Make a paper template of the contour or use a contour gauge. To use a contour gauge, press the gauge onto the profile and trace it onto the tile.

2   Use a wet saw to make a series of closely spaced, parallel cuts, then nip away the waste.

USING TILE NIPPERS

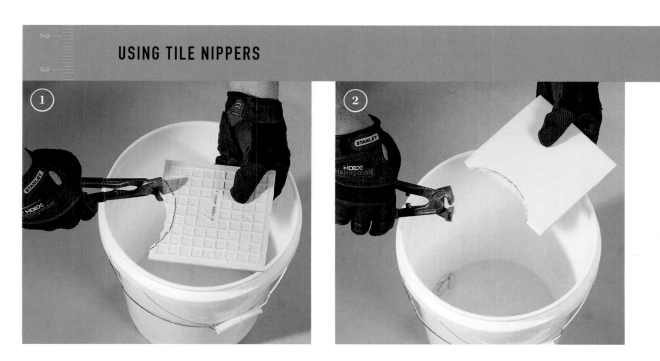

1   Tile nippers have sharp carbide tipped jaws that are used to firmly grip the leading edge of a tile and snap off small fragments of unwanted material. They are primarily used to make irregular cuts in tile.

2   To avoid breaking the tile, use the tile nippers to take very small bites out of the cut. Afterwards, use a rubbing stone to smooth the sharp edges of exposed cuts.

Cutting Mosaic Tile

1   Align the tile to be cut with the last full row of tile and butt it against the pipe. Mark the center of the pipe onto the front edge of the tile.

2   Place a ¼" spacer against the wall and butt the tile against it. Mark the pipe center on the side edge of the tile. Using a combination square, draw a line through each mark to the edges of the tile.

3   Starting from the intersection of the lines at the center, draw a circle slightly larger than the pipe or protrusion.

Score cuts on mosaic tiles with a tile cutter in the row where the cut will occur. Cut away excess strips of mosaics from the sheet, using a utility knife, then use a handheld tile cutter to snap tiles one at a time. Note: Use tile nippers to cut narrow portions of tiles after scoring.

Alternately, you can use a wet saw, in which case you do not need to cut excess pieces off the sheet. This makes it convenient to use more of each sheet.

OPTIONS FOR CUTTING HOLES IN TILES

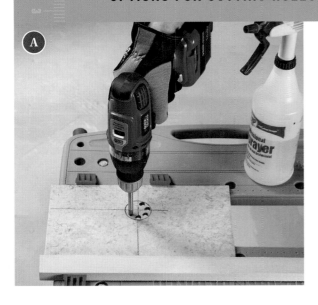

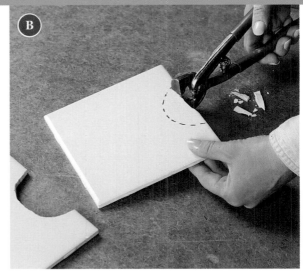

A   Drill around the edges of the hole using a ceramic tile bit. Gently knock out the waste material with a hammer. The rough edges of the hole will be covered by a protective plate (called an escutcheon).

B   Variation: Score and cut the tile so the hole is divided in half, using the straight-cut method, then use the curved-cut method to remove waste material from each half of the circle.

CUTTING A HOLE WITH A HOLE SAW

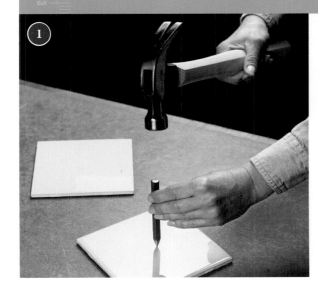

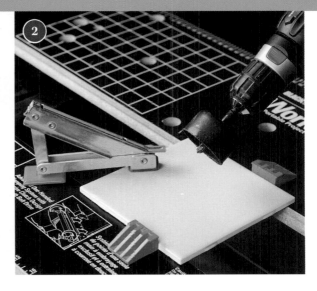

1   Make a dimple with a center punch to break through the glaze, to keep the drill bit from wandering.

2   Select a tungsten carbide hole saw in the appropriate size and attach it to a power drill. Place the tip at the marked center and drill the hole.

CUTTING CEMENTBOARD

Even though cementboard is a rigid material that breaks or crushes fairly easily, with the right tools, it can be cut to fit with little difficulty. The best way to make straight cuts in cementboard is to use a carbide scoring knife (or utility knife with heavy-duty blades) to cut shallow guidelines in the panel, which can then be snapped and broken accurately. With practice and patience, L-cuts and cutouts are also possible using this tool. This method generates no dust.

Carbide and diamond-tipped hole saws are useful for boring smaller diameter holes in tile and cementboard in order to accommodate items such as water pipe and valve protrusions. Spraying the bit with water while you are drilling will help to reduce dust and lubricate the cutting edge of the bit.

A jigsaw fitted with a carbide tungsten grit blade is a versatile power tool capable of making curved and straight cuts in cementboard. Purchase some extra blades though, as they tend to wear out quickly.

A rotary tool fitted with a tile-cutting bit is useful for making round cutouts for toilet flanges. These saws are often supplied with a circular cutting guide for making custom-sized radial cuts. With a little practice, a rotary tool (also called a spiral-cutting tool) can be used to make L-cuts and rectangular cutouts for electrical boxes. The tile cutting bits are prone to breakage due to heat and the high torque generated by the saw, so set it to a low working speed and periodically lubricate the bits with all-purpose oil.

Safety Tip
Dry-cutting tile or cementboard with any power tool will produce harmful silica dust. Wear a respirator and safety glasses while cutting and make tile and cementboard cuts outdoors in a well-ventilated area whenever possible. A fan is recommended to provide additional ventilation and to help blow dust away from the workspace.

Skillbuilder

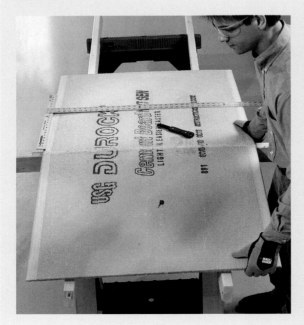

Buy a sheet of cementboard, the same type you will be using in your project. Score and snap the cementboard sheet in half by using a scoring tool. Measure and mark the rough side of the cementboard to the desired size. Using a straightedge as a guide, score the board with a carbide scoring tool, then snap the panel evenly along the scored line. Use a utility knife to cut the glass-fiber mesh layer just below the surface of the cement board.

On one of the cut pieces, cut a 2" strip off one edge. Cut wider strips until you are able to get a clean cut. This is your minimum clean cut size for doing a snap cut. During your project, any cuts smaller than this will need to be done with a jigsaw.

If your project includes hole cutouts, use the second piece to practice cutting holes of the same size as your project.

Save these scraps to use in later Skillbuilders.

MAKING STRAIGHT CUTS IN CEMENTBOARD

1   To make L-cuts in cementboard with a carbide scoring tool, mark the outline of the cut on both sides of the panel. Using a straightedge as a guide, score both sides of the panel and punch the waste material out from the back side of the panel using a hammer.

2   To make L-cuts in cementboard with a jigsaw, mark the outline of the desired cut on the panel with a pencil. Fit the jigsaw with an abrasive blade and cut out and remove the waste material.

MAKING ROUND CUTOUTS IN CEMENTBOARD

1   A power drill fitted with a carbide or diamond-tipped hole saw can be used to make round and curved cutouts. Mark the centerpoint of the cut on the panel and bore the hole at low speed. To improve performance, use a spray bottle filled with water to periodically moisten the cutting edge of the bit.

2   To use a rotary saw, fit it with a tile cutting bit, adjust the circle cutter guide to the desired hole size and drill a pilot hole in the center point and perimeter of the desired cut. Insert the pivot foot of the guide and the bit into the pilot holes and complete the cut.

3   Jigsaw for rounds cuts. To make round cuts in cementboard using a jigsaw fitted with a carbide grit blade, mark the center point of the cut on the panel and drill a starter hole. Insert the jigsaw blade into the pilot hole and complete the cut.

TILING FLOORS

PROBABLY THE MOST COMMON tile project undertaken by homeowners is the basic floor project. A floor project is a great place to start because you have fewer worries in terms of plumb walls and true corners. On the negative side, a great deal of attention needs to be paid to the condition of the subfloor and underlayment, including the often messy task of removing the existing floor covering. This chapter shows you exactly how to handle the preparations so you get the best possible results from your tiling job.

This chapter walks you through a basic installation, basement floor installation, and glass mosaic installation. All three projects are straightforward and will develop tiling skills.

A floor typically is one of the largest surfaces in a room and so plays a major role in establishing the style of the space. Take the time to look at as many tile floors as you can, in a variety of settings, to help you decide how you want your project to look.

Evaluating & Preparing Floors

THE MOST IMPORTANT STEP in the success of your tile flooring project is evaluating and preparing the area. A well-done tile installation can last a lifetime, whereas poor preparation can lead to a lifetime of cracked grout and broken tile headaches.

Because of the weight of ceramic and stone tile, it is important to assess the condition of the joists, subfloor, and underlayment. Most tile installation cannot be done over existing flooring without the addition of underlayment. Check with your tile dealer for the specific requirements of the tile or stone you have chosen.

Though it may initially seem like more work, it is important to remove bathroom fixtures, vanities, and non-plumbed kitchen islands for your floor tile project. Not only will this eliminate a great deal of cutting and fitting, it will allow you more flexibility in future remodeling choices.

Start by removing any fixtures or appliances in the work area, then baseboards, then the old flooring. Shovel old flooring debris through a window and into a wheelbarrow to speed up removal work. Cover doorways with sheet plastic to contain debris and dust during the removal process. Keep the dust and dirt from blowing through your home's ductwork by covering air and heat vents with sheet plastic and masking tape.

Anatomy of Your Floor

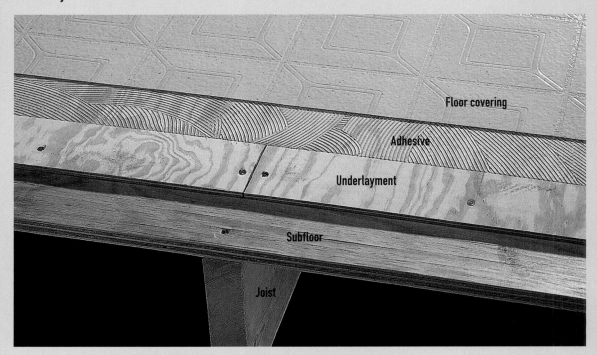

A typical wood-frame floor consists of several layers that work together to provide the required structural support and desired appearance. At the bottom of the floor are joists, the 2 × 10 or larger framing members that support the weight of the floor. Joists are typically spaced 16" apart on center. The subfloor is nailed to the joists. Most subfloors installed in the 1970s or later are made of ¾" tongue-and-groove plywood, but in older homes, the subfloor often consists of 1"-thick wood planks nailed diagonally across the floor joists. On top of the subfloor, most builders place a ½" plywood underlayment. For many types of floor coverings, adhesive or mortar is spread on the underlayment prior to installing the floor cover.

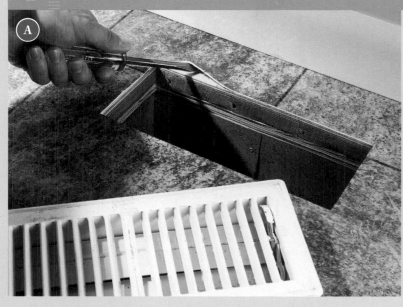

A   Removing a floor register gives you a cut away view of existing floor covering layers. This floor appears to have a plywood subfloor, tongue and groove wood flooring, ¼" plywood underlayment, and sheet vinyl. At minimum, the sheet vinyl would need to be removed, then cementboard and tile could be installed. One drawback is that this adds height to transitions between rooms. Another option would be to remove the vinyl, underlayment, and wood flooring. The new tile floor would then be about ¼" less thick than the existing floor.

B   Measure vertical spaces in kitchens and bathrooms to ensure the proper fit of appliances and fixtures after the installation of tile. Use a sample of the tile and any additional underlayment as spacers while measuring.

C   Remove baseboards using a pry bar placed against a scrap board to avoid damaging the drywall. Pry the baseboard at all nail locations. Number the baseboards as they are removed.

D   Prepare door jambs by measuring the height of your underlayment and tile and marking the casing. Using a jamb saw, cut the casing at the mark.

E   Test the height of the door jamb by sliding a piece of flooring under the door jamb to make sure it fits easily.

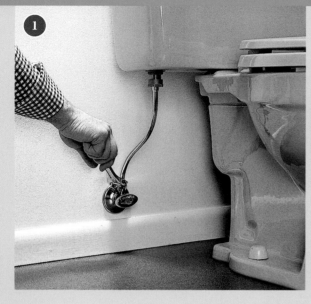

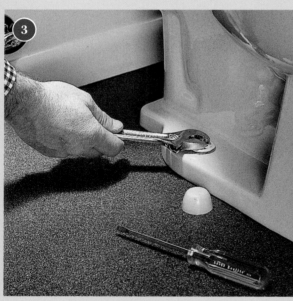

1   Empty the tank and disconnect. Turn off the water at the shutoff valve and flush the toilet to empty the tank. Use a sponge to soak up remaining water in the tank and bowl. Disconnect the supply tube using an adjustable wrench.

2   Remove the nuts from the tank bolts using a ratchet wrench. Carefully remove the tank and set it aside.

3   Pry off the floor bolt trim caps, then remove the nuts from the floor bolts. Rock the bowl from side to side to break the seal, then lift the toilet from the bolts and set it aside. Wear rubber gloves while cleaning up any water that spills from the toilet trap.

4   Scrape the old wax from the toilet flange, and plug the drain opening with a damp rag so sewer gas doesn't escape into the house. If you're going to reinstall the old toilet, clean the old wax and plumber's putty from around the horn and base of the toilet.

1 Self-rimming sink: Disconnect the plumbing, then slice through any caulk or sealant between the sink rim and the countertop using a utility knife. Lift the sink off the countertop.

2 Pedestal sink: Disconnect the plumbing. If the sink and pedestal are bolted together, disconnect them. Remove the pedestal first, supporting the sink from below with 2 × 4s. Slice through any caulk or sealant. Lift the sink off the wall brackets (inset).

3 Vanity: Detach any mounting hardware, located underneath the countertop inside the vanity.

4 Slice through any caulk or sealant between the wall and the countertop. Remove the countertop from the vanity, using a pry bar if necessary.

5 Remove the screws or nails (usually driven through the back rail of the cabinet) that anchor the vanity to the wall and remove the cabinet.

Removing Floor Coverings

Use a floor scraper to remove resilient flooring products and to scrape off leftover adhesives or backings. The long handle provides leverage and force, and it allows you to work in a comfortable standing position. A scraper will remove most flooring, but you may need to use other tools to finish the job.

Tools & Materials

Gloves
Floor scraper
Utility knife
Spray bottle
Wallboard knife
Wet/dry vacuum
Heat gun
Dust mask
Hand maul
Masonry chisel
Flat pry bar
Broom
Tape measure
End-cutting nippers
Liquid dishwashing detergent
Belt sander with coarse sanding belt
Eye and ear protection

THOROUGH AND CAREFUL removal work is essential to the quality of a new floor tile or stone installation. The difficulty of flooring removal depends on the type of floor covering and the method that was used to install it. Carpet and perimeter-bond vinyl are generally quite easy to remove, and vinyl tiles are relatively simple. Full-spread sheet vinyl can be difficult to remove, however, and removing ceramic tile is a lot of work.

With any removal project, be sure to keep your tool blades sharp and avoid damaging the underlayment if you plan to reuse it. If you'll be replacing the underlayment, it may be easier to remove the old underlayment along with the floor covering.

Resilient flooring installed before 1986 might contain asbestos, so consult an asbestos containment expert or have a sample tested before beginning removal. Even if asbestos is not present, wear a high-quality dust mask.

1   Cut strips. Remove base moldings, if necessary. Use a utility knife to cut old flooring into strips about a foot wide.

2   Pull up as much flooring as possible by hand, gripping the strips close to the floor to minimize tearing.

3   Cut stubborn sheet vinyl into strips about 5" wide. Starting at a wall, peel up as much of the floor covering as possible. If the felt backing remains, spray a solution of water and liquid dishwashing detergent under the surface layer to help separate the backing. Use a wallboard knife to scrape up particularly stubborn patches.

4   Scrape up the remaining sheet vinyl and backing using a floor scraper. If necessary, spray the backing again with the soap solution to loosen it. Sweep up the debris, then finish the cleanup with a wet/dry vacuum. Tip: Fill the vacuum with about an inch of water to help contain dust.

REMOVING VINYL TILE

1   Carefully pry tiles loose. Remove base moldings, if necessary. Starting at a loose seam, use a long-handled floor scraper to remove tiles. To remove stubborn tiles, soften the adhesive with a heat gun, then use a wallboard knife to pry up the tile and scrape off the underlying adhesive.

2   Remove stubborn adhesive or backing by wetting the floor with a water/detergent mixture, then scraping with a floor scraper.

REMOVING CERAMIC TILE

1   Knock tiles loose. Remove base moldings, if necessary. Knock out tile using a hand maul and masonry chisel. If possible, start in a space between tiles where the grout has loosened. Be careful when working around fragile fixtures, such as drain flanges.

2   If you plan to reuse the underlayment, use a floor scraper to remove any remaining adhesive. You may have to use a belt sander with a coarse sanding belt to grind off stubborn adhesive.

Variation: To remove glued-down carpet, first cut it into strips with a utility knife, then pull up as much material as you can. Scrape up the remaining cushion material and adhesive with a floor scraper.

1   Using a utility knife, cut around metal threshold strips to free the carpet. Remove the threshold strips with a flat pry bar.

2   Cut the carpet into pieces small enough to be easily removed. Roll up the carpet and remove it from the room, then remove the padding. Note: Padding is often stapled to the floor, and usually will come up in pieces as you roll it up.

3   Using end-cutting nippers or pliers, remove all staples from the floor. Pry tackless strips loose with a pry bar and remove them.

Removing Underlayment

Remove underlayment and floor covering as though they were a single layer. This is an effective removal strategy with any floor covering that is bonded to the underlayment.

Tools & Materials

Eye and ear protection
Gloves
Circular saw with carbide-tipped blade
Flat pry bar
Reciprocating saw
Wood chisel
Screwdriver
Hammer
Hand maul
Masonry chisel

Warning

This floor removal method releases flooring particles into the air. Be sure the flooring you are removing does not contain asbestos.

FLOORING CONTRACTORS

routinely remove the underlayment along with the floor covering before installing new flooring. This saves time and makes it possible to install new underlayment that is ideally suited to ceramic and stone tile. Do-it-yourselfers using this technique should make sure they cut flooring into pieces that can be easily handled.

Beware of Screwheads

Examine fasteners to see how the underlayment is attached. Use a screwdriver to expose the heads of the fasteners. If the underlayment has been screwed down, you will need to remove the floor covering and then unscrew the underlayment.

Variation: If your existing floor is ceramic tile over plywood underlayment, use a hand maul and masonry chisel to chip away the tile along the cutting lines before making the cuts.

1   Cut the flooring and underlayment. Remove base moldings, if necessary. Adjust the cutting depth of a circular saw to equal the combined thickness of your floor covering and underlayment. Using a carbide-tipped blade, cut the floor covering and underlayment into squares measuring about 3 ft. square. Be sure to wear eye protection and gloves.

2   Use a reciprocating saw to extend cuts close to the edges of walls. Hold the blade at a slight angle to the floor, and try not to damage walls or cabinets. Do not cut deeper than the underlayment. Use a wood chisel to complete cuts near cabinets.

3   Separate the underlayment from the subfloor using a flat pry bar and hammer. Remove and discard the sections of underlayment and floor covering immediately, watching for exposed nails.

Installing Underlayment

BEFORE YOU BEGIN INSTALLING CEMENTBOARD on a horizontal surface, the substructure will need to be examined to make sure it meets the requirements for a tile backer board installation. Wood subfloors installed over 16 inch on-center floor joists must be made of wood stock that is at least ⅝-inch thick and rated for floor sheathing. Acceptable sheathing includes exterior grade, tongue and groove, C-C plugged or better plywood, or oriented strand board (OSB) made with exterior glues. Floors that have large dips or bulges, or any areas with deflection problems, will require structural repairs or reinforcement. It is always recommended that you contact a structural engineer if you are unsure about the condition of your floor and support system.

Cabinet countertops require a minimum overlay of ¾-inch thick sheathing. The application of ¼-inch thick cementboard is optional for installation over countertops, as well as for floor joists spaced 16 inches on center (if the substructure is overlaid with ¾-inch thick sheathing). Unless otherwise allowed by the manufacturer, use ½-inch thick cementboard for all other applications.

Tools & Materials

6" joint knife
Eye and ear protection
2" fiberglass mesh tape
1¼" cementboard screws
¼" square notched trowel
Floor-patching compound
Latex or acrylic additive
Heavy flooring roller
Work gloves
Drill
Straightedge
Tape measure
Utility knife
Thinset mortar
Cementboard
1" deck screws
Circular saw
Power sander
Dust mask

Skillbuilder

Use the scrap cementboard from the Skillbuilder under Cutting Cementboard (p. 36) and a piece of ¾" plywood for these exercises. Mix a small batch of thinset (about 3" in the bottom of a bucket). Using the ¼" trowel, apply thinset to the plywood. Place the large pieces of cut cementboard and some of the strips onto the thinset base with ⅛" gaps between. Secure with cementboard screws. All screws should be flush with the cementboard surface or slightly below it—but not all the way through! See what happens if you try to drive a screw too close to the edge of the cementboard.

Apply thinset mortar and fiberglass tape to the joints in the cementboard. Practice your joint knife scraping skills until you get a nice smooth joint.

Using the inexpensive tiles from the Skillbuilder under Cutting Tile (p. 30), develop a layout plan to cover this sample sheet. Play around with all the possible ways tiles can be arranged—square, offset, diagonal.

Mix a fresh batch of thinset and begin laying the tiles according to the layout plans, making cuts as needed. Use spacers if you will be using spacers in your project. Practice troweling the thinset to get only as much thinset as needed to create the square ridges with the notched trowel. After laying the tile, examine each joint to see if thinset has squished up into the joint space. Remove this excess, as it will cause flaws in the grout. Remove the spacers, if you used spacers.

Mix a small batch of grout and grout your sample. Refer to steps 16 through 18 in the Installing Ceramic Floor Tile project (p. 59). Work the grout into the joints, then wipe off excess.

Admire your work! Think about how much time it took to tile your sample. Extrapolate how much time it will take to tile your desired project. Remember that most of your tiling project will entail you working on your knees. This is why it is important to tile in small sections. Tiling is physically difficult and deserves a high level of attention to detail, as it is such a permanent installation.

INSTALLING CEMENTBOARD UNDERLAYMENT

1   In most cases, cementboard should be set into a bed or layer of thinset mortar. Use a ¼" square notched trowel to spread the setting bed of dry-set or modified thinset mortar. Apply only enough thinset for each panel and then set the panel into position according to your layout lines. Set the panels with the rougher-textured side facing up.

2   Fasten panels to the subfloor with 1¼" self-piloting cementboard screws. Fasten screws every 6 to 8" in the field, keeping fasteners 2" away from each corner but no less than ⅜" from the panel edges. Properly fastened, the head of each screw will sit flush with or just slightly below the surface of the panel.

3   Add new panels, staggering the seams at adjoining panels to prevent any four corners from converging at one point. Install the cementboard perpendicular to floor joists, but avoid aligning them with existing plywood joints on the subfloor.

4   Maintain ⅛"-wide gaps between panels. Fill these gaps with a modified thinset mortar, overlapping at least 2 to 3" on each side of the juncture. Center and embed 2"-wide alkaline-resistant fiberglass tape over the joint and tightly skim thinset over the length of the abutment using a joint knife. Scrape off excess mortar to ensure an even transition between panel edges.

INSTALLING PLYWOOD UNDERLAYMENT

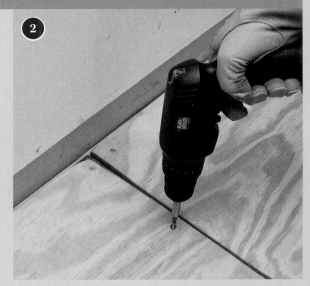

1   Begin by installing a full sheet of plywood along the longest wall, making sure the underlayment seams will not be aligned with the subfloor seams. Fasten the plywood to the subfloor, using 1" deck screws driven every 6" along the edges and at 8" intervals in the field of the sheet.

2   Continue fastening sheets of plywood to the subfloor, driving the screw heads slightly below the underlayment surface. Leave ¼" expansion gaps at the walls and between sheets. Offset seams in subsequent rows.

3   Using a circular saw or jigsaw, notch plywood to meet existing flooring in doorways, then fasten the notched sheets to the subfloor.

4   Mix floor-patching compound and latex or acrylic additive according to the manufacturer's directions. Spread it over seams and screw heads with a joint knife.

5   Let the patching compound dry, then sand the patched areas using a power sander.

INSTALLING ISOLATION MEMBRANE

1   Thoroughly clean the subfloor, then apply thinset mortar with a notched trowel. Start spreading the mortar along a wall in a section as wide as the membrane and 8 to 10 ft. long. Note: For some membranes, you must use a bonding material other than mortar. Read and follow label directions.

2   Roll out the membrane over the mortar. Cut the membrane to fit tightly against the walls using a straightedge and utility knife.

3   Starting in the center of the membrane, use a heavy flooring roller (available at rental centers) to smooth out the surface toward the edges. This frees trapped air and presses out excess bonding material.

4   Repeat steps 1 through 3, cutting the membrane as necessary at the walls and obstacles, until the floor is completely covered with membrane. Do not overlap the seams, but make sure they are tight. Allow the mortar to cure for two days before installing the tile.

Installing Ceramic Floor Tile

Tools & Materials

¼" square-notched trowel
Rubber mallet
Tile cutter
Tile nippers
Hand-held tile cutter
Needlenose pliers
Grout float
Grout sponge
Soft cloth
Thinset mortar
Tile
Tile spacers
Grout
Latex grout additive
Wall adhesive
2 × 4 lumber
Grout sealer
Tile caulk
Sponge brush
Cementboard
Chalk line
Tape measure
Drill
Caulk gun
1¼" cementboard screws
Fiberglass-mesh wallboard tape
Utility knife or grout knife
Threshold material
Jigsaw or circular saw with a
     tungsten-carbide blade
Rounded bullnose tile
Eye protection and gloves

Floor tile can be laid in many decorative patterns, but for your first effort, it may be best to stick to a basic grid. In most cases, floor tile is combined with profiled base tile (installed after flooring).

TO BEGIN A CERAMIC TILE INSTALLATION, snap perpendicular reference lines and dry-fit tiles to ensure the best placement.

When setting tiles, work in small sections so the mortar doesn't dry before the tiles are set. Use spacers between tiles to ensure consistent spacing. Plan an installation sequence to avoid kneeling on set tiles. Be careful not to kneel or walk on tiles until the designated drying period is over. Also, use kneepads or a kneeling pad to protect your knees.

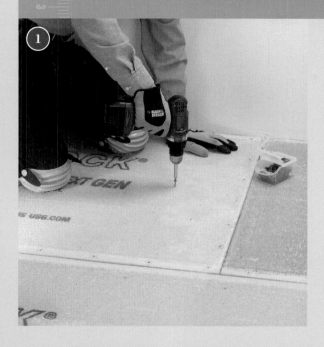

Option: Build a grid system of chalk lines based on the actual dimensions of your tiles, including the grout lines. A grid system ensures that you will stay on track and it helps you divide the project into small sections so you can apply the correct amount of thinset without guessing.

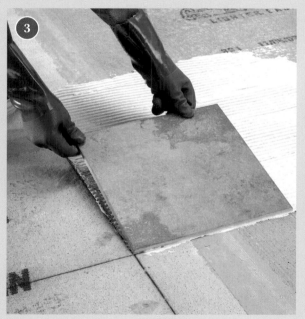

1. Fasten cementboard in place with 1¼" cementboard screws. Place fiberglass-mesh wallboard tape over the seams. Cover the remainder of the floor, following the steps on page 51.

2. Draw reference lines and establish the tile layout. Mix a batch of thinset mortar, then spread the mortar evenly against both reference lines of one quadrant, using a ¼" square-notched trowel. Use the notched edge of the trowel to create furrows in the mortar bed.

3. Set the first tile in the corner of the quadrant where the reference lines intersect. When setting tiles that are 8" square or larger, twist each tile slightly as you set it into position.

continued

Variation: For large tiles or uneven stone, use a larger trowel with notches that are at least ½" deep.

Variation: For mosaic sheets, use a ³⁄₁₆" V-notched trowel to spread the mortar and a grout float to press the sheets into the mortar. Apply pressure gently to avoid creating an uneven surface.

4   Using a soft rubber mallet, gently tap the central area of each tile a few times to set it evenly into the mortar.

5   To ensure consistent spacing between tiles, place plastic tile spacers at the corners of the set tile. With mosaic sheets, use spacers equal to the gaps between tiles.

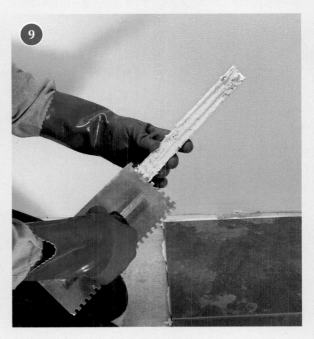

6   Position and set adjacent tiles into the mortar along the reference lines. Make sure the tiles fit neatly against the spacers.

7   To make sure the tiles are level with one another, place a straight piece of 2 × 4 across several tiles, then tap the board with a mallet.

8   Lay tile in the remaining area covered with mortar. Repeat steps 2 to 8, continuing to work in small sections, until you reach walls or fixtures.

9   Measure and mark tiles to fit against walls and into corners. Cut the tiles to fit leaving an expansion joint of about 1". Apply thinset mortar directly to the back of the cut tiles, instead of the floor, using the notched edge of the trowel to furrow the mortar.

continued

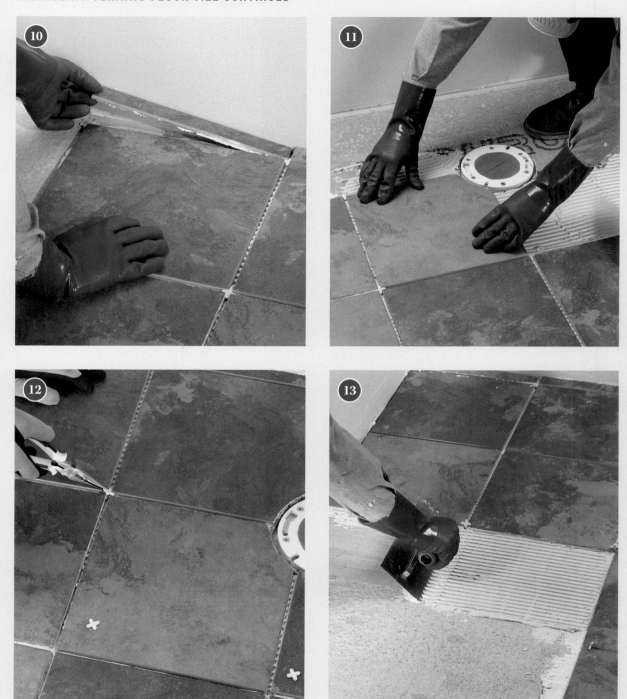

10 Set the cut pieces of tile into position. Press down on the tile until each piece is level with adjacent tiles.

11 Measure, cut, and install tiles that require notches or curves to fit around obstacles, such as exposed pipes or toilet drains.

12 Carefully remove the spacers with needlenose pliers before the mortar hardens.

13 Apply mortar and set tiles in the remaining quadrants, completing one quadrant before starting the next. Inspect all tile joints and use a utility knife or grout knife to remove any high spots of mortar that could show through the grout.

14 Install threshold material in doorways. If the threshold is too long for the doorway, cut it to fit with a jigsaw or circular saw and a tungsten-carbide blade. Set the threshold in thinset mortar so the top is even with the tile. Keep the same amount of space between the threshold as between tiles. Let the mortar set for at least 24 hours.

15 Prepare a small batch of floor grout to fill the tile joints. When mixing grout for porous tile, such as quarry or natural stone, use an additive with a release agent to prevent grout from bonding to the tile surfaces.

16 Starting in a corner, pour the grout over the tile. Use a rubber grout float to spread the grout outward from the corner, pressing firmly on the float to completely fill the joints. For best results, tilt the float at a 60° angle to the floor and use a figure eight motion.

17 Use the grout float to remove excess grout from the surface of the tile. Wipe diagonally across the joints, holding the float in a near-vertical position. Continue applying grout and wiping off excess until about 25 sq. ft. of the floor has been grouted.

continued

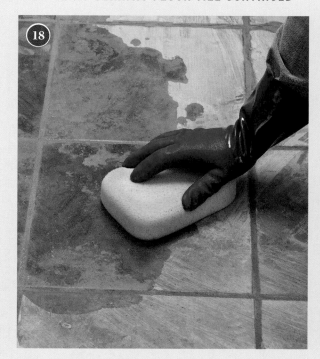

Option: Use a tile sealer to seal porous tile, such as quarry tile or unglazed tile. Following the manufacturer's instructions, roll a thin coat of sealer over the tile and grout joints using a paint roller and extension handle.

18 Wipe a damp grout sponge diagonally over about 2 sq. ft. of the floor at a time. Rinse the sponge in cool water between wipes. Wipe each area only once, since repeated wiping can pull grout back out of joints. Repeat steps 15 to 18 to apply grout to the rest of the floor.

19 Allow the grout to dry for about 4 hours, then use a soft cloth to buff the tile surface and remove any remaining grout film.

20 Apply grout sealer to the grout lines using a small sponge brush. Avoid brushing sealer onto the tile surfaces. Wipe up any excess sealer immediately.

INSTALLING BULLNOSE BASE TRIM

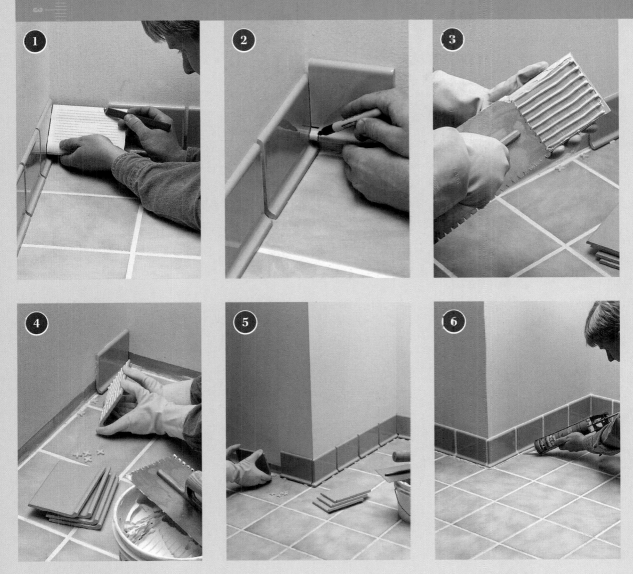

1   Dry-fit the tiles to determine the best spacing. Grout lines in base tile do not always align with grout lines in the floor tile. Use rounded bullnose tiles at outside corners, and mark tiles for cutting as needed.

2   Leaving a ⅛" expansion gap between tiles at corners, mark any contour cuts necessary to allow the coved edges to fit together. Use a jigsaw with a tungsten-carbide blade to make curved cuts.

3   Begin installing base-trim tiles at an inside corner. Use a notched trowel to apply wall adhesive to the back of the tile. Place ⅛" spacers on the floor under each tile to create an expansion joint.

4   Press the tile onto the wall. Continue setting tiles, using spacers to maintain ⅛" gaps between the tiles and ⅛" expansion joints between the tiles and floor.

5   Use a double-bullnose tile on one side of outside corners to cover the edge of the adjoining tile.

6   After the adhesive dries, grout the vertical joints between tiles and apply grout along the tops of the tiles to make a continuous grout line. Once the grout hardens, fill the expansion joint between the tiles and floor with caulk.

Installing Ceramic Tile on a Basement Floor

Tools & Materials

Sponge
Rubber mallet
Paint roller
Chalk line
Framing square
¼" notched square trowel
Needlenose pliers
Rubber grout float
Trisodium phosphate
Rubber gloves
Concrete patching compound
Concrete sealer
Grout sealer
Ceramic or stone tile
Thinset or other mortar
Grout
Spacers
Paintbrush

Ceramic, porcelain, or stone tile is impervious to water and therefore makes an excellent flooring choice for basements.

SETTING TILE OR FLAGSTONE on a concrete floor is a simple project. Its success depends on proper preparation of the concrete, a good layout, and attention to detail during the setting process. It's important to fill dips, cracks, and holes in the concrete with concrete patch or floor leveler before setting tile. If the surface is too uneven, the tile will crack under the pressure of foot traffic.

Choose tile or stone with enough texture to be a safe surface despite the moist conditions of a basement. After you've chosen the tile or stone, ask your retailer about the appropriate mortar and grout for your application.

Before establishing reference lines for your project, think about where to start tiling. The goal is to continue working without having to step on previously laid tile.

INSTALLING TILE ON A BASEMENT FLOOR

1   Test the layout by dry-setting one vertical and one horizontal row of tile all the way to the walls in both directions. If the layout results in uneven or awkward cuts at the edges, adjust the reference lines to produce a better layout.

2   Mix a batch of reinforced thinset mortar and spread it onto the floor with a ¼" square-notched trowel. Hold the trowel at a 30° angle and avoid obscuring your reference lines.

3   Set a tile into the mortar bed so it aligns with your reference lines. Rap the tile very gently with a rubber mallet to seat it in the mortar bed. Make sure it remains aligned properly. Spread mortar for the next tile, or as many as you think you can install in about 20 minutes. If your tiles do not have cast-in nibs that set the spacing automatically, use plastic tile spacers between tiles to create consistent grout gaps.

4   Butter smaller tiles that are cut to fill out the ends of runs by applying thinset mortar directly to the tile back, using a ¼" square-notched trowel. Set remaining tiles and let the mortar set up and dry for at least 24 hours before walking on the tiles.

5   Mix sanded grout according to the manufacturer's directions and fill the gaps between tiles with the grout. Use a grout float to apply the grout. Remove excess grout with a sponge and clean water after the grout film on the tile surfaces dries to a haze. Don't get too aggressive.

6   Seal the grout lines with penetrating grout sealer after the material has cured for at least a week (see manufacturer's directions). Use a sponge brush or a corner paint roller to apply the sealant.

Installing A Glass Mosaic Tile Floor

Tools & Materials

Tape measure
Chalk line
¼" notched trowel
Grout float
Grout sponge
Buff rag
Sponge applicator
Needlenose pliers
2 × 4 wrapped in carpet
Mosaic tile
Tile adhesive
Tile spacers
Grout
Grout sealer
Tile nippers
Rubber mallet
Tile cutter
Straightedge
Eye protection

THROUGHOUT HISTORY, mosaic tile has been more than a floor or wall covering—it's an art form. In fact, the Latin origins of the word mosaic refer to art "worthy of the muses." Mosaic tile is beautiful and durable, and working with it is easier than ever today. Modern mosaic floor tile is available in squares that are held together by an underlayer of fabric mesh. These squares are set in much the same way as larger tile, but their flexibility makes them slightly more difficult to hold, place, and move. The instructions given with this project simplify the handling of these squares.

The colors of mosaic tile shift just as much as any other tile, so make sure all the boxes you buy are from the same lot and batch. Colors often vary from one box to another, too, so it's a good idea to mix tile between boxes to make any shifts less noticeable.

It's also important to know that adhesive made for other tile may not work with glass or specialty mosaic tile. Consult your tile retailer for advice on the right mortar or mastic for your project. Before you start, clean and prepare the floor. Measure the room and draw reference lines. Lay out sheets of tile along both the vertical and horizontal reference lines. If these lines will produce small or difficult cuts at the edges, shift them until you're satisfied with the layout.

1   Beginning at the intersection of the horizontal and vertical lines, apply the recommended adhesive in one quadrant. Spread it outward evenly with a notched trowel. Lay down only as much adhesive as you can cover in 10 to 15 minutes.

2   Stabilize a sheet of tile by randomly inserting three or four plastic spacers into the open joints.

3   Pick up diagonally opposite corners of the square and move it to the intersection of the horizontal and vertical references lines. Align the sides with the reference lines and gently press one corner into place on the adhesive. Slowly lower the opposite corner, making sure the sides remain square with the reference lines. Massage the sheet into the adhesive, being careful not to press too hard or twist the sheet out of position. Continue setting tile, filling in one square area after another.

continued

4   When two or three sheets are in place, lay a scrap of 2 × 4 wrapped in carpet across them and tap it with a rubber mallet to set the fabric mesh into the adhesive and force out any trapped air.

5   When you've tiled up close to the wall or another boundary, lay a full mosaic sheet into position and mark it for trimming. If you've planned well and are installing small-tile mosaics, you can often avoid cutting tiles.

6   If you do need to cut tiles in the mosaic sheet, and not just the backing, score the tiles with a tile cutter. Be sure the tiles are still attached to the backing. Add spacers between the individual tiles to prevent them from shifting as you score.

7   After you've scored the tiles, cut them each individually with a pair of tile nippers.

8   Set tile in the remaining quadrants. Let the adhesive cure according to the manufacturer's instructions. Remove spacers with a needlenose pliers. Mix a batch of grout and fill the joints. Allow the grout to dry, according to manufacturer's instructions.

9   Mosaic tile has a much higher ratio of grout to tile than larger tiles do, so it is especially important to seal the grout with a quality sealer after it has cured.

Working Around Obstacles

1   To work around pipes and other obstructions, cut through the backing to create an access point for the sheet. Then, remove the tiles within the mosaic sheet to clear a space large enough for the pipe or other obstruction.

2   Set the cut sheet into an adhesive bed, and then cut small pieces of tile and fit them into the layout as necessary.

Installing A Shower Base

16d galvanized common nails
15# building paper
Staples
3-piece shower drain
PVC cement
Galvanized metal lath
Thick-bed floor mortar ("deck mud")
Latex mortar additive
Thinset mortar
CPE waterproof membrane
   & preformed dam corners
CPE membrane solvent glue
CPE membrane sealant
Cementboard and materials
   for installing cementboard
Materials for installing tile
Builder's sand
Portland cement
Masonry hoe
Gloves
Dust mask or respirator
Straightedge
¼" wood shims
Mortar
Tile spacers
Balloon tester
Silicon caulk
Caulk gun

Tools & Materials

Tape measure
Circular saw
Hammer
Utility knife
Stapler
2-ft. level
Mortar mixing box

Trowel
Wood float
Felt-tip marker
Ratchet wrench
Tin snips
Torpedo level
Tools for installing tile
Framing lumber (1×, 2 × 4, 2 × 10)

BUILDING A CUSTOM-TILED SHOWER BASE

lets you choose the shape and size of your shower rather than having its dimensions dictated by available products. Building the base is quite simple, though it does require time and some knowledge of basic masonry techniques because the base is formed primarily using mortar. What you get for your time and trouble can be spectacular.

Before designing a shower base, contact your local building department regarding code restrictions and to secure the necessary permits. Most codes require water controls to be accessible from outside the shower and describe acceptable door positions and operation. Requirements like these influence the size and position of the base.

Choosing the tile before finalizing the design lets you size the base to require mostly full tile. Showers are among the most frequently used amenities in the average home, so it really makes sense to build one that is comfortable and pleasing to your senses. Consider using small tile and gradate the color from top to bottom or in a sweep across the walls. Or, use trim tile and listellos on the walls to create an interesting focal point.

Whatever tile you choose, remember to seal the grout in your new shower and to maintain it carefully over the years. Water-resistant grout protects the structure of the shower and prolongs its useful life.

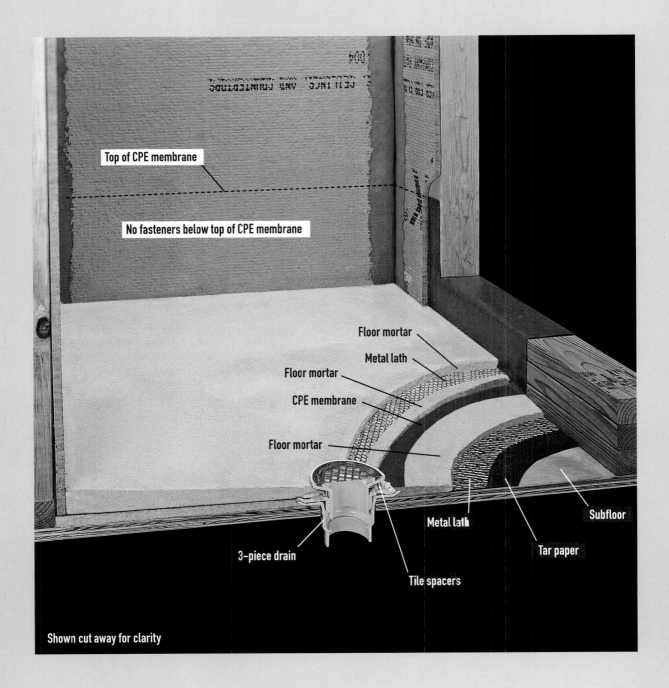

Top of CPE membrane

No fasteners below top of CPE membrane

Floor mortar

Metal lath

Floor mortar

CPE membrane

Floor mortar

3-piece drain

Metal lath

Tile spacers

Subfloor

Tar paper

Shown cut away for clarity

Tips for Building a Custom Shower Base

A custom-tiled shower base is built in three layers to ensure proper water drainage the pre-pan, the shower pan, and the shower floor. A mortar pre-pan is first built on top of the subfloor, establishing a slope toward the drain of ¼" for every 12" of shower floor. Next, a waterproof chlorinated polyethylene (CPE) membrane forms the shower pan, providing a watertight seal for the shower base. Finally, a second mortar bed reinforced with wire mesh is installed for the shower floor, providing a surface for tile installation. If water penetrates the tiled shower floor, the shower pan and sloped pre-pan will direct it to the weep holes of the 3-piece drain.

One of the most important steps in building a custom-tiled shower base is testing the shower pan after installation (step 13). This allows you to locate and fix any leaks to prevent costly damage.

1 Add the dry ingredients (builders sand and Portland cement) to a mortar box in the correct ratios. For general purposes, four parts sand to one part mortar mix (by volume) works. Don't mix more mud than you can use in a half hour or so.

2 Add small amounts of clean, potable water to the dry mixture and blend to an evenly moist consistency using a masonry hoe. Be sure to wear gloves and a dust mask or respirator.

3 A squeezed clump of deck mud should hold its shape without sagging or falling apart.

Mixing Deck Mud

Mortar beds for laying tile are made from deck mud, a simple mortar consisting of a proportioned mixture of builders sand and Portland cement, with a little water added to bind the particles together. Sometimes referred to as dry pack mortar or floor mud, it can be purchased in prepackaged blends or you can easily make it yourself. It can be set in thicker layers than ordinary thinset mortar.

Deck mud is made using a recipe consisting of a ratio of four to six parts of builders sand to one part of Portland cement. The higher the proportion of Portland cement in the mixture, the richer it is considered to be. Leaner mortars contain a lower proportion of Portland cement. A mortar bed 1¼" thick (a common thickness for a shower receptor base) requires approximately 12 pounds of dry sand per square foot of application. Add an additional three pounds of sand per square foot for each additional ¼" of mortar thickness desired. The amount of Portland cement required will depend on the mixing ratio and the total volume of sand required to complete the job. A richer blend that uses a four-to-one ratio is suitable for small areas like shower pan mortar beds.

The ingredients for making your own mortar bed "mud" are minimal. You'll need sharp sand (also called builders sand), Portland cement, and water. The proportions vary by application.

1   Remove building materials to expose subfloor and stud walls. Cut three 2 × 4s for the curb and fasten them to the floor joists and the studs at the shower threshold with 16d galvanized common nails. Also cut 2 × 10 lumber to size and install in the stud bays around the perimeter of the shower base.

2   Staple 15# building paper to the subfloor of the shower base. Disassemble the 3-piece shower drain and glue the bottom piece to the drain pipe with PVC cement. Partially screw the drain bolts into the drain piece, and stuff a rag into the drain pipe to prevent mortar from falling into the drain.

3   Mark the height of the bottom drain piece on the wall farthest from the center of the drain. Measure from the center of the drain straight across to that wall, then raise the height mark ¼" for every 12" of shower floor to slope the pre-pan toward the drain. Trace a reference line at the height mark around the perimeter of the entire alcove using a level.

4   Staple galvanized metal lath over the building paper; cut a hole in the lath ½" from the drain. Mix floor mortar (or "deck mud") to a fairly dry consistency using a latex additive for strength; mortar should hold its shape when squeezed (inset). Trowel the mortar onto the subfloor, building the pre-pan from the flange of the drain piece to the height line on the perimeter of the walls.

continued

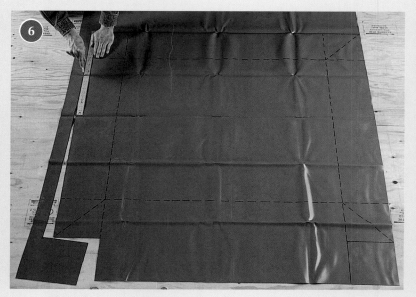

5   Continue using the trowel to form the pre-pan, checking the slope using a level and filling any low spots with mortar. Finish the surface of the pre-pan with a wood float until it is even and smooth. Allow the mortar to cure overnight.

6   Measure the dimensions of the shower floor, and mark it out on a sheet of CPE waterproof membrane using a felt-tipped marker. From the floor outline, measure out and mark an additional 8" for each wall and 16" for the curb end. Cut the membrane to size using a utility knife and straightedge. Be careful to cut on a clean, smooth surface to prevent puncturing the membrane. Lay the membrane onto the shower pan.

7   Measure to find the exact location of the drain and mark it on the membrane, outlining the outer diameter of the drain flange. Cut a circular piece of CPE membrane roughly 2" larger than the drain flange, then use CPE membrane solvent glue to weld it into place and reinforce the seal at the drain.

8   Apply CPE sealant around the drain. Fold the membrane along the floor outline. Set the membrane over the pre-pan so the reinforced drain seal is centered over the drain bolts. Working from the drain to the walls, carefully tuck the membrane tight into each corner, folding the extra material into triangular flaps.

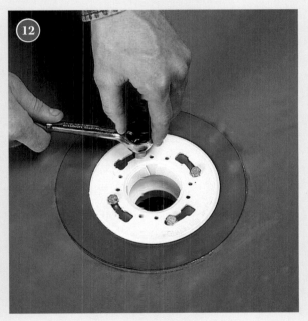

9   Apply CPE solvent glue to one side, press the flap flat, then staple it in place. Staple only the top edge of the membrane to the blocking; do not staple below the top of the curb, or on the curb itself.

10   At the shower curb, cut the membrane along the studs so it can be folded over the curb. Solvent-glue a dam corner at each inside corner of the curb. Do not fasten the dam corners with staples.

11   At the reinforced drain seal on the membrane, locate and mark the drain bolts. Press the membrane down around the bolts, then use a utility knife to carefully cut a slit just large enough for the bolts to poke through. Push the membrane down over the bolts.

12   Use a utility knife to carefully cut away only enough of the membrane to expose the drain and allow the middle drain piece to fit in place. Remove the drain bolts, then position the middle drain piece over the bolt holes. Reinstall the bolts, tightening them evenly and firmly to create a watertight seal.

continued

13 Test the shower pan for leaks overnight. Place a balloon tester in the drain below the weep holes, and fill the pan with water, to 1" below the top of the curb. Mark the water level and let the water sit overnight. If the water level remains the same, the pan holds water. If the level is lower, locate and fix leaks in the pan using patches of membrane and CPE solvent.

14 Install cementboard on the alcove walls, using ¼" wood shims to lift the bottom edge off the CPE membrane. To prevent puncturing the membrane, do not use fasteners in the lower 8" of the cementboard. Cut a piece of metal lath to fit around the three sides of the curb. Bend the lath so it tightly conforms to the curb. Pressing the lath against the top of the curb, staple it to the outside face of the curb. Mix enough mortar for the two sides of the curb.

15 Overhang the front edge of the curb with a straight 1× board, so it is flush with the outer wall material. Apply mortar to the mesh with a trowel, building to the edge of the board. Clear away excess mortar, then use a torpedo level to check for plumb, making adjustments as needed. Repeat for the inside face of the curb. Allow the mortar to cure overnight. Note: The top of the curb will be finished after tile is installed (step 19).

16 Attach the drain strainer piece to the drain, adjusting it to a minimum of 1½" above the shower pan. On one wall, mark 1½" up from the shower pan, then use a level to draw a reference line around the perimeter of the shower base. Because the pre-pan establishes the ¼" per foot slope, this measurement will maintain that slope.

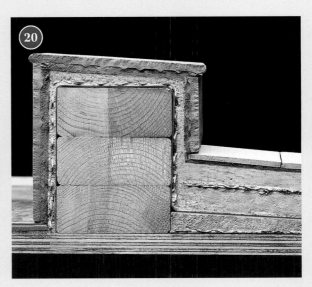

17 Spread tile spacers over the weep holes of the drain to prevent mortar from plugging the holes. Mix the floor mortar, then build up the shower floor to roughly half the thickness of the base. Cut metal lath to cover the mortar bed, keeping it ½" from the drain (see photo in step 18).

18 Continue to add mortar, building the floor to the reference line on the walls. Use a level to check the slope, and pack mortar into low spots with a trowel. Leave space at the drain for the thickness of the tile. Float the surface using a wood float until it is smooth and slopes evenly to the drain. When finished, allow the mortar to cure overnight before installing the tiles.

19 After the floor has cured, draw reference lines and establish the tile layout, then mix a batch of thinset mortar and install the floor tile. At the curb, cut the tiles for the inside to protrude ½" above the unfinished top of the curb, and the tiles for the outside to protrude ⅝" above the top, establishing a ⅛" slope so water drains back into the shower. Use a level to check the tops of the tiles for level as you work.

20 Mix enough floor mortar to cover the unfinished top of the curb, then pack it in place between the tiles using a trowel. Screed off the excess mortar flush with the tops of the side tiles. Allow the mortar to cure, then install bullnose cap tile. Install the wall tile, then grout, clean, and seal all the tile. After the grout has cured fully, run a bead of silicone caulk around all inside corners to create control joints.

TILING WALLS

TILING A WALL differs only slightly from tiling a floor. The main difference is that wall tiles are somewhat limited by size and weight. A weighty tile has to be held in place while the thinset or adhesive sets, which can be a tricky process. Another concern with walls is that they are rarely plumb and corners are rarely true. This leads to a little bit more prep work to create a good base. On the plus side, wall tiles do not have to withstand foot traffic, so the options for decorative finishes multiplies.

This chapter starts with a very basic wall project that can be adapted for many different applications. Then, we go over how to tile a tub alcove, another tile project that's frequently undertaken by do-it-yourselfers.

Evaluating & Preparing Walls

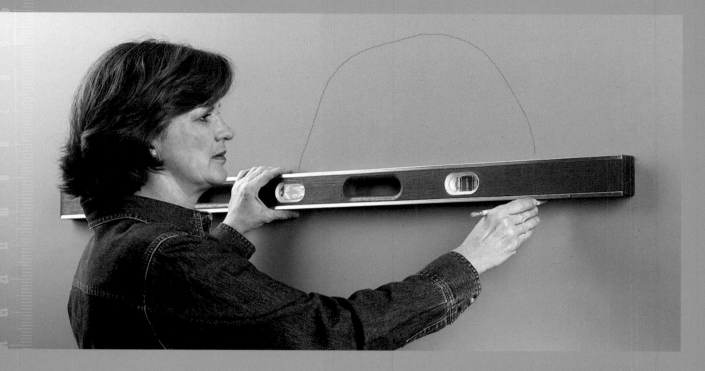

Run a straightedge up and down and side-to-side along wall surfaces and outline the valleys. Any difference of ¼" or more must be filled with joint compound using a 12" taping knife. You may need to apply a number of thin layers for best results. Some plaster surfaces are softer than others. High lime content plaster (inset) is too soft to serve as a backing surface for tile.

THE SUBSTRATE FOR WALL TILES must be stable; that is, it must not expand and contract in response to changes in temperature or humidity. For this reason, it will be necessary to strip all wallpaper before tiling, even if the paper has been painted. Similarly, remove any type of wood paneling before tiling a wall. Even painted walls need some preparation. For example, paint that's likely to peel needs to be sanded thoroughly before the project starts.

Smooth concrete walls can be tiled, but the concrete has to be prepared. Scrub it with a concrete cleaner, then apply a concrete bonding agent. Use a grinder to smooth any unevenness. Install an isolation membrane to keep the tile from cracking if the walls crack, which is a common problem.

Brick or block walls are a good substrate for tiling, but the surface is not smooth enough to be tiled

without additional preparation. Mix extra Portland cement into brick mortar, apply a smooth, even skim coat to the walls, and let it dry thoroughly before beginning the tile project.

Existing tile can be tiled over as long as the glaze has been roughened enough for the adhesive to adhere properly. Remember, though, that the new tile will protrude quite a way from the wall. You'll need to accommodate for this on the edges and around receptacles, switches, windows or doors, and other obstacles.

In some cases, you'll find that it's easiest to remove the old substrate and install new (see pages 80 to 81). Even if you're working with an appropriate substrate in good condition, you will need to evaluate the wall to make sure it is plumb and flat, and fix surface flaws before you begin your wall tiling project.

PATCHING HOLES

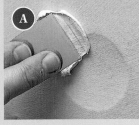
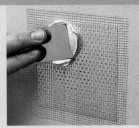

A   Patching small holes: Fill smooth holes with spackle, then sand smooth. Cover ragged holes with a repair patch, then apply two coats of spackle or wallboard compound. Use a damp sponge or wet sander to smooth the repair area, then sand when dry, if necessary.

B   Patching large holes: Draw cutting lines around the hole, then cut away the damaged area using a wallboard saw. Place plywood strips behind the opening and drive wallboard screws to hold them in place. Drive screws through the wallboard patch and into the backers. Cover the joints with wallboard tape and finish with compound.

CHECKING AND CORRECTING OUT-OF-PLUMB WALLS

1   Use a plumb bob to determine if corners are plumb. A wall more than ½" out of plumb should be corrected before tiling.

2   If the wall is out of plumb, use a long level to mark a plumb line the entire height of the wall. Remove the wall covering from the out-of-plumb wall.

3   Cut and install shims on all the studs to create a new, plumb surface for attaching backing materials. Draw arrows at the shim highpoints to mark for wallboard screw placement.

Removing Wall Surfaces

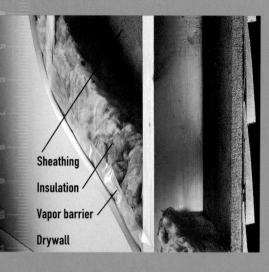

Sheathing

Insulation

Vapor barrier

Drywall

Be aware of how your wall is built before you start tearing off surfaces. If it is an exterior wall take extra care not to disturb insulation. You should plan on replacing the vapor barrier before installing new wallcoverings.

Tools & Materials

Utility knife
Pry bar
Circular saw with demolition blade
Straightedge
Maul
Masonry chisel
Heavy tarp
Reciprocating saw
    with bimetal blade
Hammer
Protective eyewear
Dust mask
2 × 4 lumber

YOU MAY HAVE TO REMOVE AND REPLACE interior wall surfaces before starting your tiling project. Most often, the material you'll be removing is wallboard, but you may be removing plaster or ceramic tile. Removing wall surfaces is a messy job, but it is not difficult. Before you begin, shut off the power and inspect the wall for wiring and plumbing.

Make sure you wear appropriate safety gear—glasses and dust masks—since you will be generating dust and small pieces of debris. Use plastic sheeting to close off doorways and air vents to prevent dust from spreading throughout the house. Protect floor surfaces and the bathtub with rosin paper securely taped down. Dust and debris will find their way under drop cloths and will quickly scratch your floor or tub surfaces.

REMOVING DRYWALL

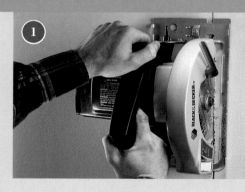

1   Remove baseboards and other trim and prepare the work area. Make a ½"-deep cut from floor to ceiling using a circular saw. Use a utility knife to finish the cuts at the top and bottom and to cut through the taped horizontal seam where the wall meets the ceiling surface.

2   Insert the end of a pry bar into the cut near one corner of the opening. Pull the pry bar until the wallboard breaks, then tear away the broken pieces. Take care to avoid damaging the wallboard outside the project area.

REMOVING PLASTER

1   Remove baseboards and other trim and prepare the work area. Score the cutting line several times with a utility knife using a straightedge as a guide. The line should be at least ⅛" deep.

2   Break the plaster along the edge by holding a scrap piece of 2 × 4 on edge just inside the scored line, and rapping it with a hammer. Use a pry bar to remove the remaining plaster.

3   Cut through the lath along the edges of the plaster using a reciprocating saw or jigsaw. Remove the lath from the studs using a pry bar.

REMOVING CERAMIC WALL TILE

1   Cover the floor with a heavy tarp, and shut off the electricity and water. Knock a small starter hole into the bottom of the wall using a maul and masonry chisel.

2   Begin cutting out small sections of the wall by inserting a reciprocating saw with a bimetal blade into the hole, and cutting along grout lines. Be careful when sawing near pipes and wiring.

3   Cut the entire wall surface into small sections, removing each section as it is cut. Be careful not to cut through studs.

Installing Cementboard on Walls

Tools & Materials

Eye and ear protection
Screw fastening bit
Stapler and staples
Modified thinset mortar
4-mil clear poly sheeting
2" fiberglass mesh tape
1¼" cementboard screws
15# roofing felt
½" cementboard
Work gloves
Drill
Tape measure
6" joint knife

Attach ½"-thick cementboard to the framing members horizontally with the rough side facing out. Use 1¼" cementboard screws. Fasten screws every 6" on-center for ceiling applications and every 8" on-center for wall applications. Keep fasteners 2" away from each corner and no less than ⅜" from the panel edges.

BEFORE YOU BEGIN WORKING, the wall and ceiling framing will need to be examined to make sure it meets the structural requirements for a backer board installation. Studs, joists, and rafters, often referred to as framing members, should be spaced a maximum of 16 inches on center for wall applications.

In wet areas, the application of a moisture barrier, 15 pound roofing felt or polyethylene film, is required to protect the wall cavity from moisture intrusion.

This is fastened directly to the framing members using staples or roofing nails. Polyethylene sheeting is commonly found in rolls that are wide enough to cover an entire wall in one piece. Asphalt roofing felt (also called building paper) is installed in lapped rows, starting from the bottom of the wall assembly. Subsequent rows should overlap the subjacent row a minimum of two inches for horizontal seams and six inches for vertical seams and corners.

PREPARING THE WALL

1   A moisture barrier consisting of 4-mil clear polyethylene sheeting can be stapled to framing members in wet areas before installing the cementboard.

2   Asphalt roofing felt (15# building paper) can also be used as a moisture barrier behind cementboard panels in wet areas.

HANGING CEMENTBOARD ON WALLS

1   Fasten panels to the wall framing members using 1¼" cementbord screws. Properly fastened, the head of each screw will sit flush with the surface of the panel. Make sure all seams fall at stud locations and install the bottom course so the panels are around ¼" off the ground.

2   Fill the joints using a modified thinset mortar and then embed fiberglass mesh tape into the mortar. Skim off excess mortar from the joint using a joint knife.

3   Complete the cementboard installation by applying thinset mortar over the tape and feathering out the edges. If you will be applying a waterproofing membrane over the cementboard surfaces, allow 24 hrs. for the thinset in the seams to dry.

Laying Out Wall Tile

Draw your tile layout to scale on the wall drawing to establish your reference lines.

ESTABLISHING PERPENDICULAR reference lines is a critical part of every tile project, including wall projects. To create these lines, measure and mark the midpoint at the top and bottom of the wall, and then again along each side. Snap chalk lines between opposite marks to create your vertical and horizontal centerlines. Use the 3-4-5 triangle method to make sure the lines are drawn correctly. Adjust the lines until they are exactly perpendicular.

Next, do a dry run of your proposed layout, starting at the center of the wall and working toward an adjoining wall. If the gap between the last full tile and the wall is too narrow, adjust your starting point. Continue to dry-fit tile along the walls, paying special attention to any windows, doors, or permanent fixtures in the wall. If you end up with very narrow tiles anywhere, adjust the reference lines (and your layout) to avoid them. It's best not to cut tiles by more than half.

If your wall has an outside corner, start your dry run there. Place bullnose tiles over the edges of the adjoining field tiles. If this results in a narrow gap at the opposite wall, install trimmed tile next to the bullnose edge to even out or avoid the gap.

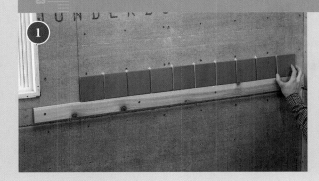

1   Attach a batten to the wall along your horizontal reference line using screws. Dry-fit tiles on the batten, aligning the middle tile with the vertical centerline.

2   If you end up with too narrow a gap along the wall in step 1, move over half the width of a tile by centering the middle tile over the vertical centerline.

3   Use a story stick to determine whether your planned layout works vertically. If necessary, adjust the size of the first row of tile.

4   Dry-fit the first row of tile, then hold a story stick along the horizontal guideline with one grout line matched to the vertical reference line. Mark the grout lines, which will correspond with the grout lines of the first row and can be used as reference points.

Tip

Check the walls and corners to see if they're plumb. Make any necessary adjustments before beginning your tile project.

Measure the walls, paying particular attention to the placement of windows, doors, and permanent fixtures. Use these measurements to create a scale drawing of each wall to be tiled.

Installing Wall Tile

Tools & Materials
Tile-cutting tools
Marker
Notched trowel
Mallet
Grout float
Grout sponge
Soft cloth
Small paintbrush or foam brush
Caulk gun
Scrap 2 × 4
Carpet
Thinset tile mortar
   with latex additive
Ceramic wall tile
Ceramic trim tile
   (as needed)
Tile grout with latex additive
Tub & tile caulk
Alkaline grout sealer
Tile spacers
⅛" shims
Eye protection

Tile is a practical, easy-to-maintain choice for bathroom walls. The variety of colors, shapes, and sizes available ensures there's a tile out there for every design and application. Keep in mind that larger tiles are easier to install, maintain, and clean than smaller tiles.

TILE IS AN IDEAL COVERING FOR WALLS,

particularly in bathrooms. Beautiful, practical, and easy to clean and maintain, tile walls are well suited to bathrooms, kitchens, mudrooms, and other hard-working spaces in your home.

When shopping for tile, keep in mind that tiles that are at least 6 × 6 inches are easier to install than small tiles, because they require less cutting and cover more surface area. Larger tiles also have fewer grout lines that must be cleaned and maintained. Check out the selection of trim and specialty tiles and ceramic accessories that are available to help you customize your project.

Most wall tile is designed to have narrow grout lines (less than ⅛-inch wide) filled with unsanded grout. Grout lines wider than ⅛-inch should be filled with sanded floor-tile grout. Either type will last longer if it contains, or is mixed with, a latex additive. To prevent staining, it's a good idea to seal your grout after it fully cures, then once a year thereafter.

You can use standard drywall or water-resistant drywall (called "greenboard") as a backer for walls in dry areas. In wet areas, install tile over cementboard. Made from cement and fiberglass, cementboard cannot be damaged by water, though moisture can pass through it. To protect the framing, install a waterproof membrane, such as roofing felt or polyethylene sheeting, between the framing members and the cementboard. Be sure to tape and finish the seams between cementboard panels before laying the tile.

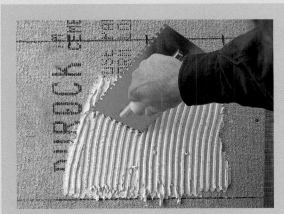

Variation: Spread adhesive on a small section of the wall, then set the tiles into the adhesive. Thinset adhesive sets fast, so work quickly if you choose this installation method.

1   Design the layout and mark the reference lines. Begin installation with the second row of tiles above the floor. If the layout requires cut tiles for this row, mark and cut the tiles for the entire row at one time.

2   Mix a small batch of thinset mortar containing a latex additive. (Some mortar has additive mixed in by the manufacturer and some must have additive mixed in separately.) Cover the back of the first tile with adhesive, using a ¼" notched trowel.

3   Beginning near the center of the wall, apply the tile to the wall with a slight twisting motion, aligning it exactly with the horizontal and vertical reference lines. When placing cut tiles, position the cut edges where they will be least visible.

continued

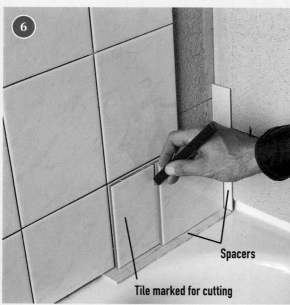

Spacers

Tile marked for cutting

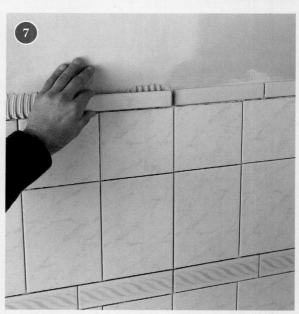

4   Continue installing tiles, working from the center to the sides in a pyramid pattern. Keep the tiles aligned with the reference lines. If the tiles are not self-spacing, use plastic spacers inserted in the corner joints to maintain even grout lines. The base row should be the last row of full tiles installed. Cut tile as necessary.

5   As small sections of tile are completed, set the tile by laying a scrap of 2 × 4 wrapped with carpet onto the tile and rapping it lightly with a mallet. This embeds the tile solidly in the adhesive and creates a flat, even surface.

6   To mark bottom and edge row tiles for straight cuts, begin by taping ⅛" spacers against the surfaces below and to the side of the tile. Position a tile directly over the last full tile installed, then place a third tile so the edge butts against the spacers. Trace the edge of the top tile onto the middle tile to mark it for cutting.

7   Install any trim tiles, such as the bullnose edge tiles shown above, at border areas. Wipe away excess mortar along the top edges of the edge tiles. Use bullnose and corner bullnose (with two adjacent bullnose edges) tiles at outside corners to cover the rough edges of the adjoining tiles.

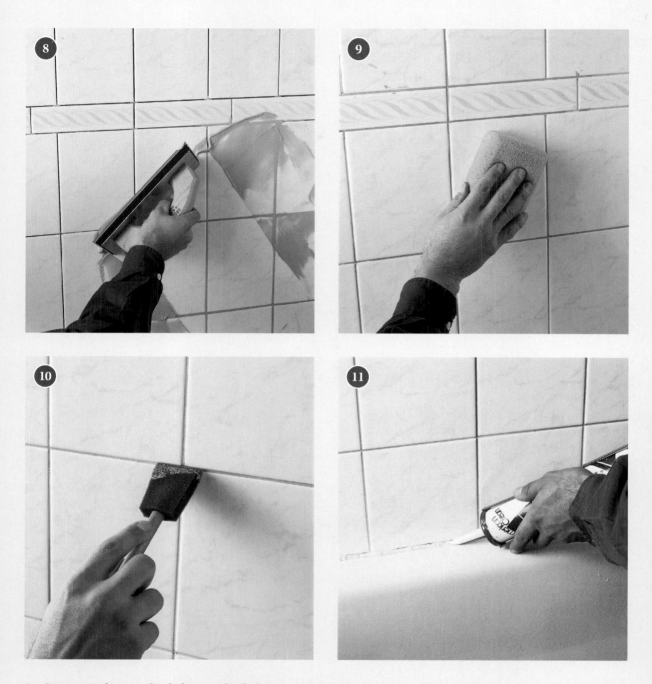

8   Let mortar dry completely (12 to 24 hrs.), then mix a batch of grout containing latex additive. Apply the grout with a rubber grout float, using a sweeping motion to force it deep into the joints. Do not grout joints adjoining bathtubs, floors, or room corners. These will serve as expansion joints and will be caulked later.

9   Wipe a damp grout sponge diagonally over the tile, rinsing the sponge in cool water between wipes. Wipe each area only once; repeated wiping can pull grout from the joints. Allow the grout to dry for about 4 hrs., then use a soft cloth to buff the tile surface and remove any remaining grout film.

10 When the grout has cured completely, use a small foam brush to apply grout sealer to the joints, following the manufacturer's directions. Avoid brushing sealer on the tile surfaces, and wipe up excess sealer immediately.

11 Seal expansion joints at the floor and corners with silicone caulk. After the caulk dries, buff the tile with a soft, dry cloth.

Installing a Tile Tub Surround

Before

4-mil polyethylene sheeting
6" joint knife
Cardboard
Caulk gun
Drill
Eye and ear protection
Square notched trowel
Modified thinset mortar
Stapler and staples
Carbide scoring tool
Carbide hole saw bit
Grout release agent
Grout float
Grout
Grout sponge
Keyhole saw
Latex tile caulk
Tape measure
Tarps
Tile
Tile-cutting tools
Trim tile
Work gloves
Utility knife
Screwdriver
Hammer
Wood blocking
Tile spacers
Small roller
Caulk gun

Tools & Materials

1 × 2 furring strips
1¼" cementboard screws

½" cementboard
2" fiberglass mesh tape
4-ft. level

WITH A NEARLY LIMITLESS SELECTION of styles, colors, and sizes of tile to choose from, a tub tile surround replacement is an ideal home improvement project. It can transform your bathroom into a luxurious retreat, while increasing the value of your home.

Tub tile surrounds can be broken down to three basic components. The back wall is always tiled first. The towel bar wall contains the optional posts and rod used for hanging bath towels. Lastly, the manifold wall contains the valve stems, shower head, and tub spout. Some tub surrounds are topped off with a low hanging ceiling. If this is the case for

your project, install the cementboard on the ceiling first and tile the ceiling after the walls have been tiled. Ceiling tile is often installed on a diagonal pattern to avoid alignment issues with the wall tile joints.

With proper care and maintenance, nearly any type of wall or floor tile can be used for a surround. Tiles that are rated vitrified or impervious, however, absorb less moisture and are better suited for wet areas. Unglazed tiles such as the tile installed in this project may be used, but be sure to seal them well with at least two coats of tile sealant.

While field tile is estimated and purchased by the total number of square feet, trim tile such as bullnose or cap tile is quantified in linear feet. If the tile you select isn't available with matching trim tile, consider making your own using a wet tile saw fitted with a bevel profile wheel. Through-body porcelain tile is an excellent choice for making custom trim because the surface color is uniform throughout the body of the tile. Most tiled surrounds include bath accessories such as a soap dish and towel bar fixtures. Some tile families offer these accessories in the same patterns and colors. In other cases, you'll have to choose a similar—or perhaps contrasting—style or color. Make sure the thickness of the base for these accessories matches the tile thickness.

To introduce a splash of color to an otherwise plain tile surround, consider adding one or more bands of contrasting tile into the installation. Some tile product lines are available in a variety of solid colors, allowing the installer to incorporate colored rows of similarly sized tiles into the installation without having to make special adjustments to the layout. For added effect, you can even match the trim color to the colored bands of tile or sprinkle some decorative accent tiles throughout the tile installation.

A perfectly functional alcove bathtub surround (page 90) can be utterly transformed with tile (page 91).

1　Remove the old fittings. To begin, remove the tub spout, faucet handles, and shower head. Then, slice and remove the caulk from the corner joints. Existing ceramic fittings such as soap dishes should also be removed to prevent them from falling later and damaging the tub. Use a utility knife to remove old caulk, grout, and adhesive from around the lip of the tub. Finally, lay protective cardboard over the exposed surfaces of the tub and drape tarps over cabinets and toilets.

2　Cut out old surround panels or tiles. A keyhole or drywall saw can be used to safely cut through the drywall at the junction where it meets the surround. Use the edge of the tile or panel as a guide, taking care to feel for and avoid plumbing or other unseen obstacles hidden within the wall cavity.

3　Remove any wall surface material in the new tile installation area. This will need to be replaced with cementboard. Remove all nails and debris from the framing members. If necessary, install additional wood blocking to accommodate the cementboard installation.

4　Install a moisture barrier. Fasten 4-mil clear polyethylene sheeting to the studs using staples. This step may be omitted if a waterproofing membrane will be applied over the surface of the cementboard later.

5   Install ½"-thick cementboard horizontally on the back wall first, and then on the side walls. Fasten the panels to the studs using 1¼" cementboard screws. To make straight cuts, score the panel using a carbide scoring tool, then snap the panel along the scored line. To make hole cuts for plumbing protrusions, use a drill fitted with a carbide hole saw bit.

6   Fill the gaps between cementboard panels with thinset mortar, overlapping at least 2 to 3" on each side of the joint. Center and embed 2"-wide alkaline-resistant fiberglass tape over the joint and lightly skim thinset over the joint.

7   Dry-lay tile for your surround on a flat surface, inserting ⅛" spacers between the tiles to set the gap. Lay out enough for roughly half the surround height and then measure the length of the dry-laid row to find the actual height of the tiles on the wall.

8   Draw horizontal reference lines on the wall using a 4-ft. level to make sure the lines are level. Extend these reference lines to each side wall. Measure down from the horizontal lines to the tub at several points on all walls to make sure the tub deck and the lines are parallel. If they aren't, re-measure from the point where the tub deck is highest and transfer level lines all around from that point.

continued

9   Draw a vertical reference line down the center of the back wall. To temporarily support the weight of the tile that will be installed above, align and fasten 1 × 2 furring strips just below the horizontal reference lines located in the midsection of the tub surround.

10 Set the first tiles. Mix a small batch of thinset mortar. Apply the thinset using a ¼" square-notched trowel held at a 45º angle. Spread the adhesive within the guidelines on the wall, aligning the ridges of the setting bed in a horizontal direction. Install tile on the back wall first, keeping tile aligned to the centered guide line.

11 Install two or three rows of tiles—here, a row of decorative accent tiles is installed as well.

12 To mark tiles for straight cuts, place a full tile directly on top of the field tile that is installed adjacent to the void. Position another full tile over the void, abutting the overhanging edge of the tile against a ⅛" spacer. Trace the edge of this tile to mark the underlying tile for cutting.

13 Complete the upper sections. After the top portion of the back wall is tiled, fill in the upper portions of each side wall. Leave out tiles as needed to accommodate tiled-in accessories such as a soap dish or towel rod.

14 Mark and cut tiles to fit around the valve stems and water pipes as required to install your tub spout, diverter, and shower head (often, shower heads are installed above the tiles). Finish tiling the lower portions of the tile installation, then allow to dry for 24 hrs. Tip: Tape tiles together to prevent slippage while they dry.

15 Coat the tile surfaces with a sealer or other grout-release agent if they are not glazed by the manufacturer. This treatment will prevent grout from getting into places where it should not go.

16 Grout the tiles (see page 89). To apply grout, hold the grout float at an angle and force the mortar into the joints, skimming excess grout from the tile surface with each pass. Wipe tile clean using a damp grout sponge. After grouting, buff tile surfaces with a soft cloth to remove haze. Install fittings and hardware, and caulk around the tub deck.

TILING
COUNTERTOPS
& BACKSPLASHES

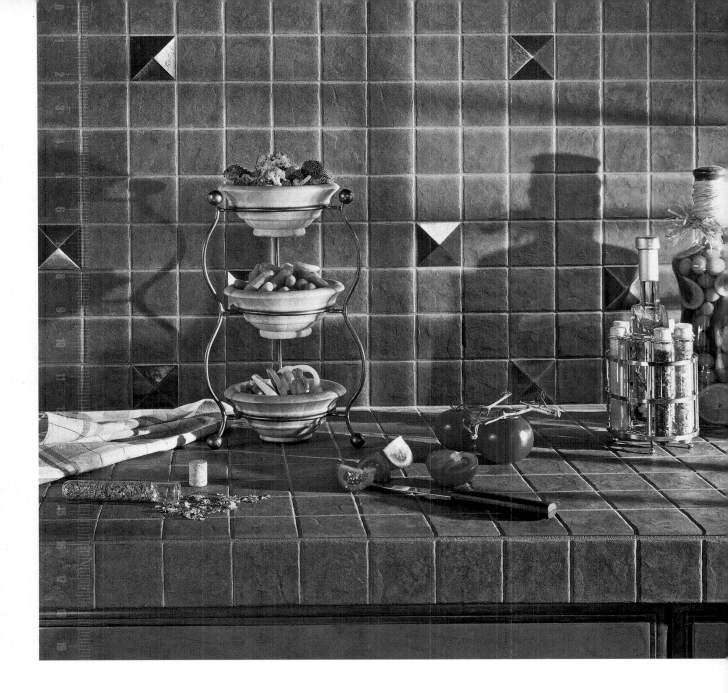

TILE COUNTERTOPS are a cook's dream—resistant to heat and stains, easy to clean, and extremely durable. Fortunately, the process of building one is much easier than most people would imagine. The projects included in this chapter lead you through constructing the countertop itself as well as tiling it.

Edge treatments are integral parts of a countertop design. Consider trim tile, wood, and other materials for your edges and create a layout that complements the treatment you choose.

When designing a countertop, remember that larger tiles produce fewer grout lines to keep clean and more stable surfaces. For work areas, flat tiles are better than tiles with rounded or beveled edges because bowls and pans rock on rounded edges.

Before selecting natural stone tile for countertops, research your choice carefully. Some natural stone stains and scratches easily and requires more maintenance than you might wish to invest in a countertop. Be especially careful about choosing porous stone, which is difficult to keep clean in a kitchen or bathroom environment.

A tile backsplash creates an easy-to-clean wall surface in the kitchen, while providing virtually millions of design options.

Tiling a Countertop

Ceramic or porcelain tile makes a durable countertop that is heat-resistant and relatively easy for a DIYer to create. By using larger tiles, you minimize the number of grout lines (and the cleaning that goes with them).

Tools & Materials

Tape measure
Circular saw
Drill with masonry bit
Utility knife
Straightedge
Stapler
Drywall knife
Framing square
Notched trowel
Grout float
Sponge
Corner bracket
Caulk gun
Ceramic tile
Tile spacers
¾" (CDX) plywood
4-mil polyethylene sheeting
Packing tape
½" cementboard
1¼" deck screws
Fiberglass mesh tape
Thinset mortar
Grout
Silicone caulk
Silicone grout sealer
Cementboard screws
Metal ruler
Eye protection
Wood scraps
Wet tile saw (available for rent)

Skillbuilder

Refer to the Skillbuilder under Underlayment (p. 50) and practice the skills if you haven't already.

Because countertop tiling requires working around edges, practice this additional skill: Apply cementboard, fiberglass tape, and tiles to the face and three edges of a 2-foot-long piece of 2 × 12 lumber. This will give you practice handling the special needs of tiling these edges.

THE BEST TILE FOR MOST COUNTERTOPS

is glazed ceramic or porcelain floor tile. Glazed tile is better than unglazed because of its stain resistance, and floor tile is better than wall tile because it is thicker and more durable. While glaze protects tile from stains, the porous grout between tiles is still quite vulnerable. To minimize staining, use a grout that contains a latex additive or mix your own grout using a liquid latex additive. After the grout cures fully, apply a quality grout sealer, and reapply the sealer once a year thereafter. Also, choosing larger tiles reduces the number of grout lines to maintain. Although the selection is a bit limited, if you choose 13 × 13-inch floor tile, you can span from the front to the back edge of the countertop with a single seam.

The countertop in this project has a substrate of ¾-inch exterior-grade plywood that's cut to fit and fastened to the cabinets. The plywood is covered with a layer of plastic (for a moisture barrier) and a layer of ½-inch-thick cementboard. The overall thickness of the finished countertop is about 1½ inches. Two layers of ¾-inch exterior-grade plywood without cementboard is also an acceptable substrate. You can purchase tiles made specifically to serve as backsplashes and front edging or cut your own edging and backsplash tiles from field tiles.

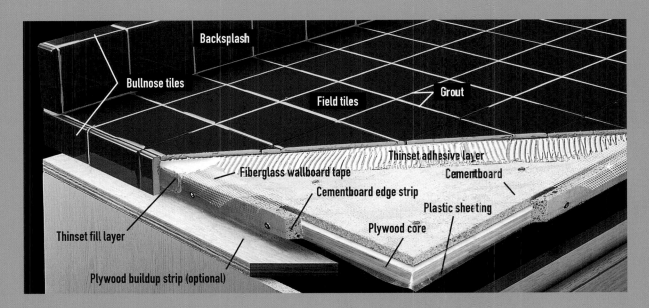

A **ceramic tile countertop** made with wall or floor tile starts with a core of ¾" exterior-grade plywood that's covered with a moisture barrier of 4-mil polyethylene sheeting. Half-inch cementboard is screwed to the plywood, and the edges are capped with cementboard and finished with fiberglass mesh tape and thinset mortar. Tiles for edging and backsplashes may be bullnose or trimmed from the factory edges of field tiles.

Options for Backsplashes & Countertop Edges

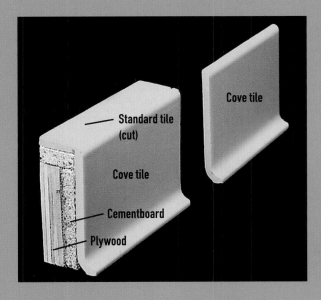

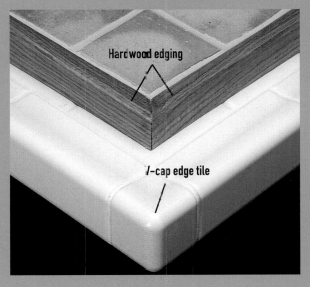

Backsplashes can be made from cove tile attached to the wall at the back of the countertop. You can use the tile alone or build a shelf-type backsplash using the same construction as for the countertop. Attach the plywood backsplash to the plywood core of the countertop. Wrap the front face and all edges of the plywood backsplash with cementboard before laying tile.

Edge options include V-cap edge tile and hardwood strip edging. V-cap tiles have raised and rounded corners that create a ridge around the countertop perimeter—good for containing spills and water. V-cap tiles must be cut with a wet saw. Hardwood strips should be prefinished with at least three coats of polyurethane finish. Attach the strips to the plywood core so the top of the wood will be flush with the faces of the tiles.

Tips for Laying Out Tile

You can lay tile over a laminate countertop that's square, level, and structurally sound. Use a belt sander with 60- or 80-grit sandpaper to rough up the surface before setting the tiles. The laminate cannot have a no-drip edge.

If you're using a new substrate and need to remove your existing countertop, make sure the base cabinets are level front to back, side to side, and with adjoining cabinets. Unscrew a cabinet from the wall and use shims on the floor or against the wall to level it, if necessary.

Installing battens along the front edge of the countertop helps ensure the first row of tile is perfectly straight. For V-cap tiles, fasten a 1 × 2 batten along the reference line using screws. The first row of field tile is placed against this batten. For bullnose tiles, fasten a batten that's the same thickness as the edging tile, plus ⅛" for mortar thickness, to the face of the countertop so the top is flush with the top of the counter. Bullnose tiles should be aligned with the outside edge of the batten. For wood edge trim, fasten a 1 × 2 batten to the face of the countertop so the top edge is above the top of the counter. The tiles are installed against the batten.

Before installing any tile, lay out the tiles in a dry run using spacers. If your counter is L-shaped, start at the corner and work outward. Otherwise, start the layout at a sink to ensure equally sized cuts on both sides of the sink. If necessary, shift your starting point so you don't end up cutting tile segments that are too narrow.

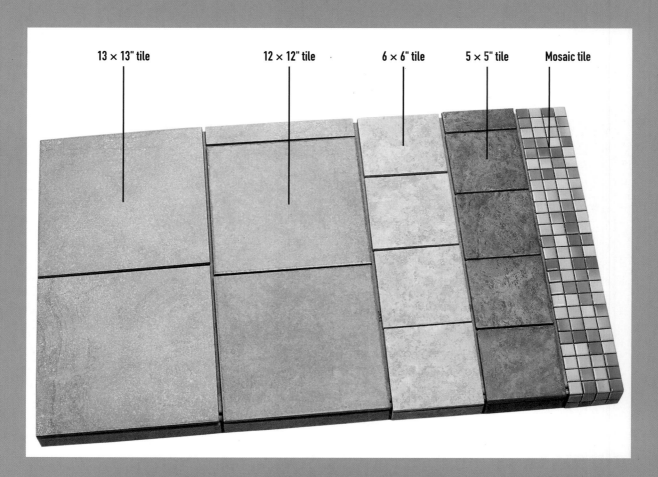

13 × 13" tile   12 × 12" tile   6 × 6" tile   5 × 5" tile   Mosaic tile

The bigger the tile the fewer the grout lines. If you want a standard 25"-deep countertop, the only way to get there without cutting tiles is to use mosaic strips or 1" tile. With 13 × 13" tile, you need to trim 1" off the back tile but have only one grout line front to back. As you decrease the size of your tiles, the number of grout lines increases.

BUILDING A TILE COUNTERTOP

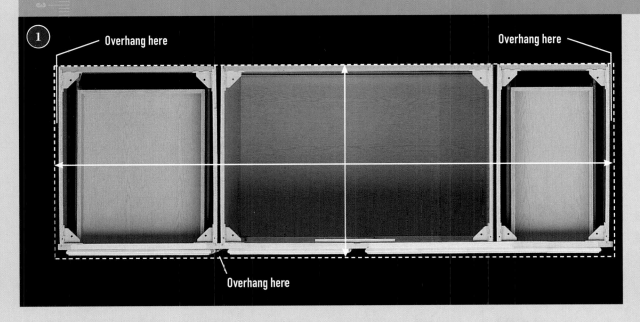

1

Overhang here

Overhang here

Overhang here

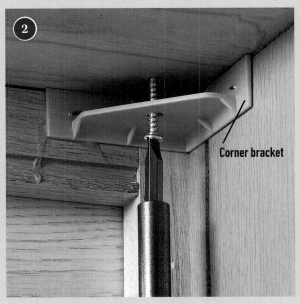

2

3

Corner bracket

1   Determine the size of the plywood substrate by measuring across the top of the cabinets. The finished top should overhang the drawer fronts by at least ¼". Be sure to account for the thickness of the cementboard, adhesive, and tile when deciding how large to make the overhang. Cut the substrate to size from ¾" plywood using a circular saw. Also make any cutouts for sinks and other fixtures.

2   Set the plywood substrate on top of the cabinets, and attach it with screws driven through the cabinet corner brackets. The screws should not be long enough to go through the top of the substrate.

3   Cut pieces of cementboard to size, then mark and make the cutout for the sink. Dry-fit them on the plywood core with the rough sides of the panels facing up. Leave a ⅛" gap between the cementboard sheets and a ¼" gap along the perimeter.

continued

Option: Cut cementboard using a straightedge and utility knife or a cementboard cutter with a carbide tip. Hold the straightedge along the cutting line, and score the board several times with the knife. Bend the piece backward to break it along the scored line. Back-cut to finish.

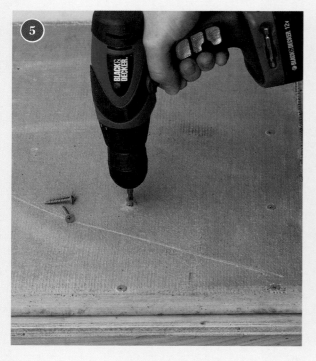

4   Lay the plastic moisture barrier over the plywood substrate, draping it over the edges. Tack it in place with a few staples. Overlap seams in the plastic by 6", and seal them with packing tape.

5   Lay the cementboard pieces rough-side up on top of the moisture barrier and attach them with cementboard screws driven every 6". Drill pilot holes using a masonry bit, and make sure all screw heads are flush with the surface. Wrap the countertop edges with 1¼"-wide cementboard strips, and attach them to the core with cementboard screws.

6   Tape all cementboard joints with fiberglass mesh tape. Apply three layers of tape along the front edge where the horizontal cementboard sheets meet the cementboard edging.

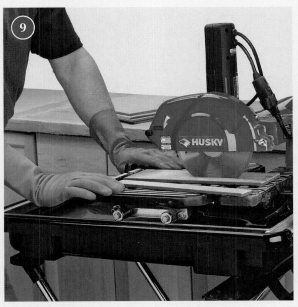

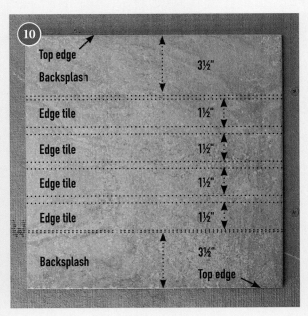

Top edge

Backsplash   3½"

Edge tile   1½"

Edge tile   1½"

Edge tile   1½"

Edge tile   1½"

Backsplash   3½"

Top edge

7   Fill all the gaps and cover all of the tape with a layer of thinset mortar. Feather out the mortar with a drywall knife to create a smooth, flat surface.

8   Determine the required width of the edge tiles. Lay a field tile onto the tile base so it overhangs the front edge by ½". Hold a metal ruler up to the underside of the tile and measure the distance from it to the bottom of the subbase. The edge tiles should be cut to this width (the gap for the grout line causes the edge tile to extend the subbase that conceals it completely).

9   Cut edge tiles to the determined width using a wet saw. It's worth renting a quality wet saw for tile if you don't own one. Floor tile is thick and difficult to cut with a hand cutter (especially porcelain tiles).

10   Cut tiles for the backsplash. The backsplash tiles (3½" wide in our project) should be cut with a factory edge on each tile that will be oriented upward when they're installed. You can make efficient use of your tiles by cutting edge tiles from the center area of the tiles you cut to make the backsplash.

continued

Sink cutout area

11 Dry-fit tiles on the countertop to find the layout that works best. Once the layout is established, make marks along the vertical and horizontal rows. Draw reference lines through the marks and use a framing square to make sure the lines are perpendicular.

Small Floor Tiles & Bullnose Edging

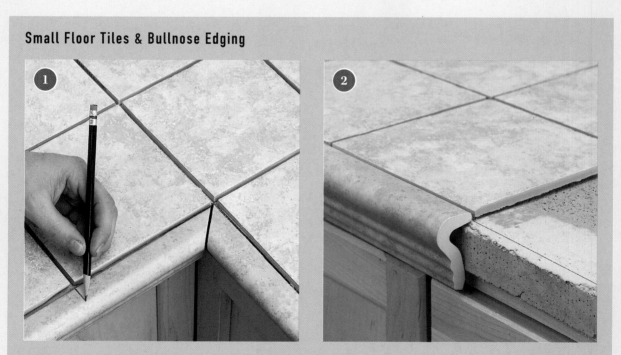

1 Lay out tiles and spacers in a dry run. Adjust the starting lines, if necessary. If using battens, lay the field tile flush with the battens, then apply the edge tile. Otherwise, install the edging first. If the countertop has an inside corner, start there by installing a ready-made inside corner or by cutting a 45° miter in the edge tile to make your own inside corner.

2 Place the first row of field tile against the edge tile, separating the tile with spacers. Lay out the remaining rows of tile. Adjust the starting lines if necessary to create a layout using the smallest number of cut tiles.

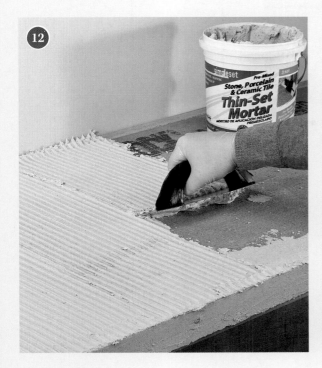

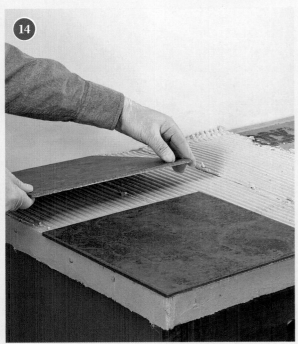

Option: To maintain even grout lines, some beginning tilers insert plus-sign-shaped plastic spacers at the joints. This is less likely to be useful with large tiles like those shown here, but it is effective. Many tiles today feature built-in spacing lugs, so the spacers are of no use. Make sure to remove the spacers before the thinset sets. If you leave them in place they will corrupt your grout lines.

12 Use a ⅜" square notched trowel to apply a layer of thinset mortar to the cementboard. Apply enough for two or three tiles, starting at one end. Hold the trowel at roughly a 30° angle and try not to overwork the mortar or remove too much.

13 Set the first tile into the mortar. Hold a piece of the edge against the countertop edge as a guide to show you exactly how much the tile should overhang the edge.

14 Cut all the back tiles for the layout to fit (you'll need to remove about 1" of a 13 × 13" tile) before you begin the actual installation. Set the back tiles into the thinset, maintaining the gap for grout lines created by the small spacer nubs cast into the tiles. If your tiles have no spacer nubs, see the option.

continued

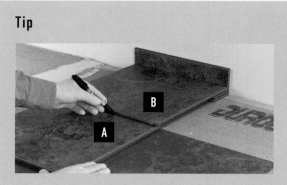

Tip

To mark border tiles for cutting, allow space for the backsplash tiles, grout, and mortar by placing a tile against the back wall. Set another tile (A) on top of the last full tile in the field, then place a third tile (B) over tile (A) and hold it against the upright tile. Mark and cut tile (A) and install it with the cut edge toward the wall. Finish filling in your field tiles.

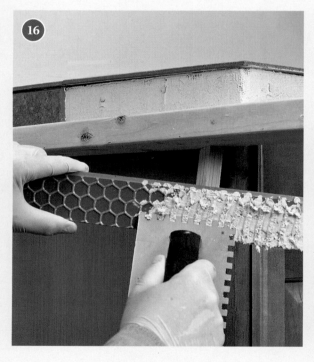

15 To create a support ledge for the edge tiles, prop pieces of 2 × 4 underneath the front edge of the substrate overhang using wood scraps to prop the ledge tightly up against the substrate.

16 Apply a thick layer of thinset to the backside of the edge tile with your trowel. This is called "buttering" and it is easier and neater than attempting to trowel adhesive onto the countertop edge. Press the tiles into position so they are flush with the leading edges of the field tiles.

17 Butter each backsplash tile and press it into place, doing your best to keep all of the grout lines aligned. Allow the mortar to set according to the manufacturer's recommendations.

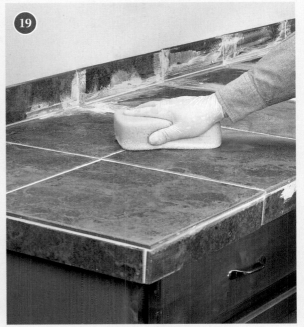

18 Mix a batch of grout to complement the tile (keeping in mind that darker grout won't look dirty as quickly as lighter grout). Apply the grout with a grout float.

19 Let the grout dry until a light film is created on the countertop surface, then wipe the excess grout off with a sponge and warm, clean water. See grout manufacturer's instructions on drying tiles and polishing.

20 Run a bead of clear silicone caulk along the joint between the backsplash and the wall. Install your sink and faucet after the grout has dried (and before you use the sink, if possible).

21 Wait at least one week and then seal the grout lines with a penetrating grout sealer. This is important to do. Sealing the tiles themselves is not a good idea unless you are using unglazed tiles (a poor choice for countertops, however).

Tiling a Backsplash

Contemporary glass mosaic sheets create a counter-to-cabinet backsplash for a waterproof, splash-proof wall with high visual impact.

Tools & Materials

Level
Tape measure
Pencil
Tile cutter
Notched trowel
Rubber grout float
Rubber mallet
Sponge
Story stick
Tile spacers (if needed)
Wall tile
Mastic adhesive
Masking tape
Grout
Caulk
Drop cloth
Caulk gun
Scrap 2 × 4
Carpet scrap
Buff cloth

THERE ARE FEW SPACES

in your home with as much potential for creativity and visual impact as the space between your kitchen countertop and your cupboards. A well-designed backsplash can transform the ordinary into the extraordinary. Tiles for the backsplash can be attached directly to wallboard or plaster and do not require backerboard. When purchasing the tile, order 10 percent extra to cover breakage and cutting. Remove the switch and receptacle coverplates and install box extenders to make up for the extra thickness of the tile. Protect the countertop from scratches by covering it with a drop cloth during the installation.

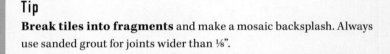

Tip

Break tiles into fragments and make a mosaic backsplash. Always use sanded grout for joints wider than ⅛".

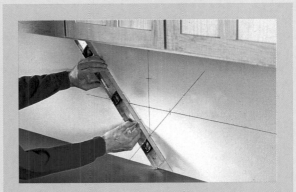

Variation: Diagonal Layout. Mark vertical and horizontal reference lines, making sure the angle is 90°. To establish diagonal layout lines, measure out equal distances from the crosspoint, and then connect the points with a line. Additional layout lines can be extended from these as needed.

1   Make a story stick by marking a board at least half as long as the backsplash area to match the tile spacing.

2   Starting at the midpoint of the installation area, use the story stick to make layout marks along the wall. If an end piece is too small (less than half a tile), adjust the midpoint to give you larger, more attractive end pieces. Use a level to mark this point with a vertical reference line.

3   While it may appear straight, your countertop may not be level and therefore is not a reliable reference line. Run a level along the counter to find the lowest point on the countertop. Mark a point two tiles up from the low point and extend a level line across the entire work area.

continued

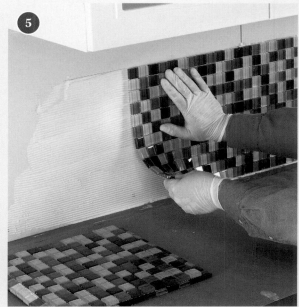

4   Apply mastic adhesive evenly to the area beneath the horizontal reference line using a notched trowel. Comb the adhesive horizontally with the notched edge.

6   Press tiles into the adhesive with a slight twisting motion. If the tiles are not self-spacing, use plastic spacers to maintain even grout lines. If the tiles do not hang in place, use masking tape to hold them in place until the adhesive sets.

6   Install a whole row along the reference line, checking occasionally to make sure the tiles are level. Continue installing tiles below the first row, trimming tiles that butt against the countertop as needed.

7   Install an edge border if it is needed in your layout. Mosaic sheets normally do not have bullnose tiles on the edges, so if you don't wish to see the cut edges of the outer tiles, install a vertical column of edge tiles at the end of the backsplash area.

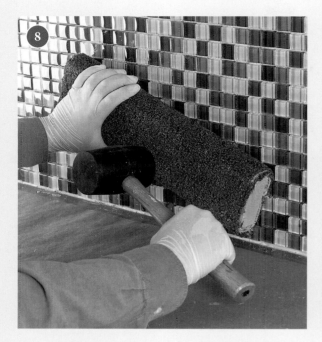

8   When the tiles are in place, make sure they are flat and firmly embedded by laying a beating block against the tile and rapping it lightly with a mallet. Remove the spacers. Allow the mastic to dry for at least 24 hours, or as directed by the manufacturer.

9   Mix the grout and apply it with a rubber grout float. Spread it over the tiles, keeping the float at a low 30° angle, pressing the grout deep into the joints. Note: For grout joints ⅛" and smaller, be sure to use a non-sanded grout.

10   Wipe off excess grout, holding the float at a right angle to the tile, working diagonally so as not to remove grout from the joints.

11   Clean excess grout with a damp sponge. When the grout has dried to a haze, buff the tile clean with a soft cloth. Apply a bead of caulk between the countertop and the tiles.

TILING
OUTDOORS

TILE MAKES AS MUCH SENSE in your outdoor home as it does indoors. Its durability, ease of maintenance, and attractive appearance bring good things to patios, gardens, and outdoor kitchens, to name just a few places.

Tile set into a mortar bed can make a very durable exterior surface, but in colder climates with significant freeze/thaw cycles the tile will not last as well. It does not take much moisture in the tile or the bed to cause tile popouts or cracking when the temperature dips. In a cold climate you will likely have better luck installing tile by bonding it to a sturdy concrete subbase (patio or steps) with exterior-rated construction adhesive. You may need to re-glue a tile occasionally, but you will have much less trouble with popouts and fracturing. Use tinted latex caulk between the tiles instead of sanded grout.

Tiling Steps

Skillbuilder

If you haven't already practiced the Skillbuilder in the Underlayment section (p. 50), do so before starting this project. Skip the cementboard and simply use a sheet of ¾" plywood. Practice the layout and tile setting portions.

Thinset mortar with latex
    bonding adhesive
Isolation membrane
Tile spacers
Buckets
Plastic sheeting
Field tile
Bullnose tile
Grout
Latex tile caulk
Grout sealer
2 × 4 lumber
Carpet scrap
Cold chisel or flat-head screwdriver
Wire brush
Broom or vacuum
Chalk
Eye protection

Tools & Materials

Pressure washer
Masonry trowel
4-ft. level
Straightedge
Tape measure
Tile cutter or wet saw

Tile nippers
Square-notched trowel
Needlenose pliers
Grout float
Grout sponge
Caulk gun
Masonry patching compound

IN ADDITION to the traditional tricks for improving your home's curb appeal—landscaping, fresh paint, pretty windows—a tiled entry makes a wonderful, positive impression. To be suitable for tiling, stair treads must be deep enough to walk on safely. Check local building codes for specifics, but most require that treads be at least 11 inches deep (from front to back) after the tile is added.

Before you start laying any tiles, the concrete must be free of curing agents, clean, and in good shape. Make necessary repairs and give them time to cure. An isolation membrane can be applied before the tile. This membrane can be a fiberglass sheet or it can be brushed on as a liquid to dry. In either case, the membrane separates the tile from the concrete, which allows the two to move independently or protects the tile from cracking due to settling or shifting of the concrete.

Choose exterior-rated, unglazed floor tile with a skid-resistant surface. Tile for the walking surfaces should be at least ½-inch thick. Use bullnose tiles at the front edges of treads (as you would on a counter-top) and use cove tiles as the bottom course on risers.

TILING CONCRETE STEPS

Option: If damage is located at a front edge, clean it as described above. Place a board in front and block the board in place with bricks or concrete blocks. Wet the damaged area and fill it with patching compound. Use a masonry trowel to smooth the patch and then allow it to cure thoroughly.

1   Use a pressure washer to clean the surface of the concrete. Use a washer with at least 4,000 psi and follow manufacturer's instructions carefully to avoid damaging the concrete with the pressurized spray.

2   Dig out rubble in large cracks and chips using a small cold chisel or flat-head screwdriver. Use a wire brush to loosen dirt and debris in small cracks. Sweep the area or use a wet/dry vacuum to remove all debris.

3   Fill small cracks and chips with masonry patching compound using a masonry trowel. Allow the patching compound to cure according to manufacturer's directions.

4   Test the surface of the steps and stoop for low spots using a 4-ft. level or other straightedge. Fill any low spots with patching compound and allow the compound to cure thoroughly.

continued

5   Apply a layer of isolation membrane over the concrete using a notched trowel. Smooth the surface of the membrane using the flat edge of a trowel. Allow the membrane to cure according to manufacturer's directions.

6   The sequence is important when tiling a stairway with landing. The primary objective is to install the tile in such a way that the fewest possible cut edges are visible from the main viewing position. If you are tiling the sides of concrete steps, start laying tile there first. Begin by extending horizontal lines from the tops of the stair treads back to the house on the sides of the steps. Use a 4-ft. level.

7   Mix a batch of thinset mortar with latex bonding adhesive and trowel it onto the sides of the steps, trying to retain visibility of the layout lines. Because the top steps are likely more visible than the bottom steps, start on top and work your way down.

8   Begin setting tiles into the thinset mortar on the sides of the steps. Start at the top and work your way downward. Try to lay out tile so the vertical gaps between tiles align. Use spacers if you need to.

9   Wrap a 2 × 4 in old carpet and drag it back and forth across the tile surfaces to set them evenly. Don't get too aggressive—you don't want to dislodge all of the thinset mortar.

10 Measure the width of a riser, including the thickness of the tiles you've laid on the step sides. Calculate the centerpoint and mark it clearly with chalk or a high visibility marker.

11 Dry-lay the tiles on the stair risers. Because the location of the tops of the riser tiles affects the positioning of the tread and landing tiles, you'll get the most accurate layout if the riser tiles are laid first. Start by stacking tiles vertically against the riser. (In some cases, you'll only need one tile to reach from tread to tread.) Add spacers. Trace the location of the tread across the back of the top tile to mark it for cutting.

12 Cut enough tiles to size to lay tiles for all the stair risers. Be sure to allow enough space for grout joints if you are stacking tiles.

13 Trowel thinset mortar mixed with bonding adhesive onto the faces of the risers. In most cases, you should be able to tile each riser all at once.

14 Lay tiles on the risers. The bottom tile edges can rest on the tread, and the tops of the top tiles should be flush with or slightly lower than the plane of the tread above.

continued

15 Dry-lay tile in both directions on the stair landing. You'll want to maintain the same grout lines that are established by the riser tiles, but you'll want to evaluate the front-to-back layout to make sure you don't end up with a row of tiles that is less than 2" or so in thickness.

16 Cut tiles as indicated by your dry run, and then begin installing them by troweling thinset mortar for the bullnose tiles at the front edge of the landing. The tiles should overlap the top edges of the riser tiles, but not extend past their faces.

17 Set the first row of field tiles, maintaining an even gap between the field tiles and the bullnose tiles.

18 Add the last row of tiles next to the house and threshold, cutting them as needed so they are between ¼ and ½" away from the house.

19 Install tiles on the stair treads, starting at the top tread and working your way downward. Set a bullnose tile on each side of the centerline and work your way toward the sides, making sure to conceal the step-side tiles with the tread tiles.

20 Fill in the field tiles on the stair treads, being sure to leave a gap between the back tiles and the riser tiles that's the same thickness as the other tile gaps.

21 Let the thinset mortar cure for a few days, and then apply grout in the gaps between tiles using a grout float. Wipe away the grout after it clouds over. Cover with plastic, in the event of rain.

22 After a few weeks, seal the grout lines with an exterior-rated grout sealer.

23 Select (or have prepared) a pretinted caulk that's the same color as your grout. Fill the gap between the back row of tiles and the house with caulk. Smooth with a wet finger if needed.

Tiling a Patio

This compact tile patio creates a welcoming entry without consuming too much yard and garden space.

Tools & Materials

Tape measure
Pencil
Chalk line
Tile cutter or wet saw
Tile nippers
Square-notched trowel
2 × 4 padded with carpet
Paintbrush and roller

Hammer
Grout float
Grout sponge
Cloth
Caulk gun
Tile spacers
Buckets
Plastic sheeting
Thinset mortar

Modular tile
Grout
Grout additive
Grout sealer
Tile sealer
Foam brush
Trowel
Eye protection

OUTDOOR TILE can be made of several different materials and is available in many colors and styles. Make sure the tiles you select are intended for outdoor use. A popular trend is to use natural stone tiles with different shapes and complementary colors, as demonstrated in this project. Tile manufacturers may offer brochures giving you ideas for modular patterns that can be created from their tiles.

When laying a modular, geometric pattern with tiles of different sizes, it's crucial that you test the layout before you begin and that you place the first tiles very carefullly. The first tiles will dictate the placement of all other tiles in your layout.

You can pour a new masonry slab on which to install your tile patio, but another option is to finish an existing slab by veneering it with tile—the scenario demonstrated here.

Outdoor tile must be installed on a clean, flat, and stable surface. When tiling an existing concrete slab, the surface must be free of flaking, wide cracks, and other major imperfections. A damaged slab can be repaired by applying a one- to two-inch-thick layer of new concrete over the old surface before laying tile.

Wear eye protection when cutting tile and handle cut tiles carefully—the cut edges of some materials may be very sharp.

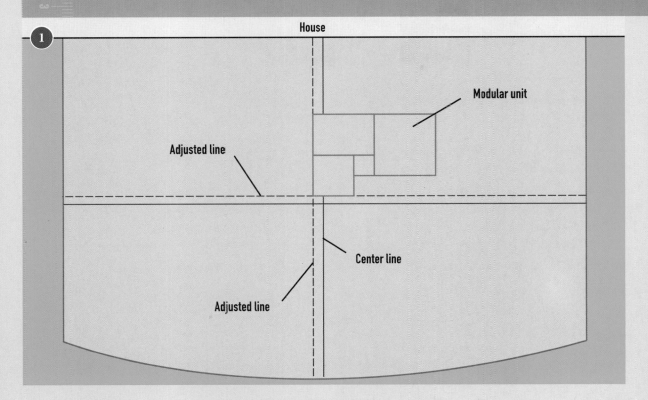

1   To establish a layout for tile with a modular pattern, you must carefully determine the location of the first tile. On the clean and dry concrete surface, measure and mark a centerline down the center of the slab. Test-fit tiles along the line—because of the modular pattern used here, the tiles are staggered. Mark the edge of a tile nearest the center of the pad, then create a second line perpendicular to the first and test-fit tiles along this line.

2   Make adjustments as needed so the modular pattern breaks evenly over the patio surface, and is symmetrical from side to side. You may need to adjust the position of one or both lines. The intersection of the lines is where your tile installation will begin. Outline the position of each group of tiles on the slab.

continued

Variation: To establish a traditional grid pattern, test-fit rows of tiles so they run in each direction, intersecting at the center of the patio. Adjust the layout to minimize tile cutting at the sides and ends, then mark the final layout and snap chalk lines across the patio to create four quadrants. As you lay tile, work along the chalklines and in one quadrant at a time.

3   Following manufacturer's instructions, mix enough thinset mortar to work for about 2 hrs. (start with 4 to 5" deep in a 5-gal. bucket). At the intersection of the two layout lines, use a notched trowel to spread thinset mortar over an area large enough to accommodate the layout of the first modular group of tiles. Hold the trowel at a 45° angle to rake the mortar to a consistent depth.

4   Set the first tile, twisting it slightly as you push it into the mortar. Align it with both adjusted layout lines, then place a padded 2 × 4 over the center of the tile and give it a light rap with a hammer to set the tile.

5   Position the second tile adjacent to the first with a slight gap between them. Place spacers on end in the joint near each corner and push the second tile against the spacers. Make certain the first tile remains aligned with the layout lines. Set the padded 2 × 4 across both tiles and tap to set. Use a damp cloth to remove any mortar that squeezes out of the joint or gets on tile surfaces. Joints must be at least ⅛"-deep to hold grout.

6   Lay the remaining tiles of the first modular unit using spacers to set gaps. Using a trowel, scrape the excess mortar from the concrete pad in areas you will not yet be working to prevent it from hardening and interfering with tile installation.

7   With the first modular unit set, continue laying tile following the pattern established. You can use the chalk lines for general reference, but they will not be necessary as layout lines. To prevent squeeze-out between tiles, scrape a heavy accumulation of mortar ½" away from the edge of a set tile before setting the adjacent tile.

Cutting Contours in Tile

To make convex (left) or concave (right) curves, mark the profile of the curve on the tile, then use a wet saw to make parallel straight cuts, each time cutting as close to the marked line as possible. Use a tile nippers to break off small portions of tabs, gradually working down to the curve profile. Finally, use an angle grinder to smooth off the sharp edges of the tabs. Make sure to wear a particle mask when using the tile saw and wear sturdy gloves when using the nippers.

continued

8   After installing the tile, remove all the spacers, cover the tiled area with plastic, and let the thinset mortar cure according to the manufacturer's instructions. When tile has fully set, remove the plastic and mix grout, using a grout additive instead of water. Grout additive is especially important in outdoor applications, because it creates joints that are more resilient in changing temperatures.

9   Use a grout float to spread grout over an area that is roughly 10 sq. ft. Push down with the face of the float to force grout into the joints, then hold the float edge at a 45° angle to the tile surfaces and scrape off the excess grout.

10   Once you've grouted this area, wipe off the grout residue using a damp sponge. Wipe with a light, circular motion— you want to clean tile surfaces but not pull grout out of the joints. Don't try to get the tile perfectly clean the first time. Wipe the area several times, rinsing out the sponge frequently.

Some tiles, such as slate, have highly porous surfaces that can be badly stained by grout. For these tiles, apply grout by filling an empty caulk tube (available at tile stores and some building centers) with grout, and apply the grout to the joints with a caulk gun. Cut the tip to make an opening just large enough to allow grout to be forced out. Run the tip down the joint between tiles as you squeeze out the grout. Remove the grout that gets on the tile surface with a wet sponge. You may need to use your finger to force grout into the joint—protect your skin by wearing a heavy glove to do this.

11   Once the grout has begun to set (usually about 1 hr., depending on temperature and humidity), clean the tile surfaces again. You want to thoroughly clean grout residue from tile surfaces because it is difficult to remove once it has hardened. Buff off a light film left after final cleaning with a cloth.

12   Cover the pad with plastic and let the grout cure according to manufacturer's instructions. Once the grout has cured, use a foam brush to apply grout sealer to only the grout, wiping any spill-over off of tile surfaces.

13   Apply tile sealer to the entire surface using a paint roller. Cover the patio with plastic and allow the sealer to dry completely before exposing the patio to weather or traffic.

Metric Conversions

Metric Equivalent

Inches (in.)	1/64	1/32	1/25	1/16	1/8	1/4	3/8	2/5	1/2	5/8	3/4	7/8	1	2	3	4	5	6	7	8	9	10	11	12	36	39.4
Feet (ft.)																								1	3	3 1/12
Yards (yd.)																									1	1 1/12
Millimeters (mm)	0.40	0.79	1	1.59	3.18	6.35	9.53	10	12.7	15.9	19.1	22.2	25.4	50.8	76.2	101.6	127	152	178	203	229	254	279	305	914	1,000
Centimeters (cm)							0.95	1	1.27	1.59	1.91	2.22	2.54	5.08	7.62	10.16	12.7	15.2	17.8	20.3	22.9	25.4	27.9	30.5	91.4	100
Meters (m)																								.30	.91	1.00

Converting Measurements

To Convert:	To:	Multiply by:		To Convert:	To:	Multiply by:
Inches	Millimeters	25.4		Millimeters	Inches	0.039
Inches	Centimeters	2.54		Centimeters	Inches	0.394
Feet	Meters	0.305		Meters	Feet	3.28
Yards	Meters	0.914		Meters	Yards	1.09
Miles	Kilometers	1.609		Kilometers	Miles	0.621
Square inches	Square centimeters	6.45		Square centimeters	Square inches	0.155
Square feet	Square meters	0.093		Square meters	Square feet	10.8
Square yards	Square meters	0.836		Square meters	Square yards	1.2
Cubic inches	Cubic centimeters	16.4		Cubic centimeters	Cubic inches	0.061
Cubic feet	Cubic meters	0.0283		Cubic meters	Cubic feet	35.3
Cubic yards	Cubic meters	0.765		Cubic meters	Cubic yards	1.31
Pints (U.S.)	Liters	0.473 (Imp. 0.568)		Liters	Pints (U.S.)	2.114 (Imp. 1.76)
Quarts (U.S.)	Liters	0.946 (Imp. 1.136)		Liters	Quarts (U.S.)	1.057 (Imp. 0.88)
Gallons (U.S.)	Liters	3.785 (Imp. 4.546)		Liters	Gallons (U.S.)	0.264 (Imp. 0.22)
Ounces	Grams	28.4		Grams	Ounces	0.035
Pounds	Kilograms	0.454		Kilograms	Pounds	2.2
Tons	Metric tons	0.907		Metric tons	Tons	1.1

Converting Temperatures

Convert degrees Fahrenheit (F) to degrees Celsius (C) by following this simple formula: Subtract 32 from the Fahrenheit temperature reading. Then mulitply that number by 5/9. For example, 77°F - 32 = 45. 45 × 5/9 = 25°C.

To convert degrees Celsius to degrees Fahrenheit, multiply the Celsius temperature reading by 9/5, then add 32. For example, 25°C × 9/5 = 45. 45 + 32 = 77°F.

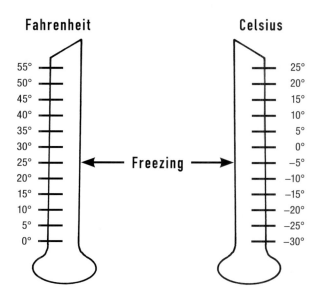

Index

First published in 2013 by Cool Springs Press, an imprint of the Quayside Publishing Group,
400 First Avenue North, Suite 400, Minneapolis, MN 55401

Cool Springs Press titles are also available at discounts in bulk quantity for industrial or sales-promotional use. For details write to Special Sales Manager at Cool Springs Press, 400 First Avenue North, Suite 400, Minneapolis, MN 55401 USA. To find out more about our books, visit us online at www.coolspringspress.com.

Library of Congress Cataloging-in-Publication Data

Homeskills. Ceramic tile : how to install ceramic tile for your floors, walls, backsplashes & countertops.
   pages cm
 Includes index.
 ISBN 978-1-59186-580-3 (softcover)
 1. Tiles--Amateurs' manuals. 2. Tile laying--Amateurs' manuals. 3. Flooring, Tile--Amateur's manuals. I. Title: Home skills. Ceramic tile. II. Title: Ceramic tile.

 TH8531.H66 2013
 693'.3--dc23

               2013004052

Design Manager: Cindy Samargia Laun
Design and layout: Danielle Smith
Cover and series design: Carol Holtz

Printed in China
10 9 8 7 6 5 4

NOTICE TO READERS

For safety, use caution, care, and good judgment when following the procedures described in this book. The publisher cannot assume responsibility for any damage to property or injury to persons as a result of misuse of the information provided.

The techniques shown in this book are general techniques for various applications. In some instances, additional techniques not shown in this book may be required. Always follow manufacturers' instructions included with products, since deviating from the directions may void warranties. The projects in this book vary widely as to skill levels required: some may not be appropriate for all do-it-yourselfers, and some may require professional help.

Consult your local building department for information on building permits, codes, and other laws as they apply to your project.